RED SOX
UNIVERSITY

RED SOX UNIVERSITY

BASEBALL'S FOREMOST INSTITUTION OF HIGHER LEARNING

ANDY WASIF

TRIUMPH
B O O K S

Library of Congress Cataloging-in-Publication Data
Wasif, Andy
    Red Sox university : baseball's foremost institution of higher
learning / Andy Wasif.
        p. cm.
ISBN 978-1-60078-218-3
1. Boston Red Sox (Baseball team)—Miscellanea. I. Title.
GV875.B62W35 2009
796.357'640974461—dc22

                                                          2008046800

This book is available in quantity at special discounts for your group or
organization. For further information, contact:

Triumph Books
542 South Dearborn Street
Suite 750
Chicago, Illinois 60605
(312) 939-3330
Fax (312) 663-3557

Printed in U.S.A.

ISBN: 978-1-60078-218-3

Design by Sue Knopf

Illustrations by Vito Sabsay

Photos courtesy of AP Images unless otherwise indicated.

For Red Sox fans everywhere

Contents

Orientation

Established in 1901 when it was known as Red Stockings University, our institution is steeped in tradition. In fact, our school shares genealogical roots with John Harvard himself. As the legend goes, after a night of binge drinking at Ye Olde Cask & Flagon, owned at the time by Sam Adams' great-great-grandfather, Adam Adams, Harvard "wrote his name in the snow" on the very spot where Red Sox University now stands.

Located near the Fens in the prestigious Back Bay section of Boston, our students attend courses in the prestigious classrooms of this prestigious institution. One might think that using the word *prestigious* several times in one sentence is simply a ploy intended to elevate the school's standing in the eyes of the reader. That's a very prestigious thought, and Red Sox University appreciates your circumspection. The fact that Red Sox fans are a skeptical and discerning bunch is gladly embraced by RSU.

Our **Motto**, *Fervidus Rabidus Fanaticus,* can be loosely translated from the Latin as "Fervid Rabid Fanatical." The staff and faculty of RSU believe in that idea and insist that their students live up to it. They ask for an open mind, a love of education, and a passion for that olde towne teame, the...who? That's right, the Boston Red Sox! (If you got that answer wrong, you might have to read the book twice.)

Helpful upperclassmen demonstrate for the Boston police what typical Red Sox fan behavior looks like.

The University welcomes **Guest Professors** with knowledge to share and a desire to teach. In the past, our classrooms have provided a forum for such luminaries as the late great Ned Martin, who lectured on Broadcasting; Carlton Fisk, whose class on Body English was highly attended; Carl Everett, who taught students how to transform their serenity into rage during his Anger Management course; and Walpole Joe Morgan, whose Magic class was popular for a time until it became clear that even he couldn't guess which card students had picked.

Our **Student Body** consists of more than 13 million full-time enrollees; the number of part-time students depends on how well the team is doing.

A large percentage of our **International Students** hail from Latin America and Japan, among other areas, to root on their favorite players.

The university is a liberal arts institution granting **Degrees** in all matters of fandom including second-guessing, scorekeeping, and Yankees-mocking.

Our **Application Deadline** is the same date that pitchers and catchers report to spring training.

RSU's **Required SAT Scores** are comparable to most schools but much higher than Lakers Fan University, the New York Institute of Yankees Fans, the Raiders Remedial Vocational School, and Colts College at South Bend.

Our **School Year** includes Spring, Summer, and, hopefully, Fall sessions. RSU also offers an exchange program in which students can spend the winter on our Florida campus.

Our **Graduation Rate** is 100 percent, making us the only university in the nation where everyone graduates. Graduates have gone on to successful careers in all sports occupations, including talk-show callers, umpire correctors, banner makers, and wave starters.

Our **Core Curriculum** encompasses Biology, History, Architecture, Government, Statistics & Probability, Economics, Health, Literature, Philosophy, and Religion. Instruction in each discipline is designed to educate new fans as well as enlighten die-*hahd* fans. For those of you who have been following the team your entire life, Red Sox University will teach you things you never knew; things you knew but didn't know you knew; things you didn't know but thought you knew; things you knew you knew but didn't know that the school knew, too; and things that were never known but are now available for knowing.

Our Mission

The preeminent institution in Red Sox Nation, Red Sox University employs a "Leave No Fan Behind" philosophy. We believe that anyone willing to learn is perfectly suited for our intensive course curriculum.

Being a Red Sox fan carries with it great responsibility. You are known throughout the major leagues as being the most knowledgeable and passionate of all fans. And that requires a constant drive to learn.

RSU celebrates the diversity of all fans and welcomes fans of all aptitudes and levels of passion. No one here will be ostracized for being less of a fan than a fellow student; everyone is pushing toward the same goal—another World Series championship. And like any team striving for that goal, fans play just as important a role in the team's success as the players do (except in the literal sense, of course). It takes every row to make the wave go, just as it takes every Red Sox fan to drown out an anti-Boston chant when playing the Yankees in New York.

Bostonians have come a long way as fans. They've seen the lowest lows and have reached the highest highs. In 2009 the age-old struggle has been replaced by a search for identity. Boston is now the one and *only* "Titletown." (That's not to be confused with "Titletown" in Detroit, "Titletown" in Green Bay, "Titletown" in Gainesville, or any of the other cities that qualify as "Titletown.") But there are children celebrating their second birthday who have never seen the Red Sox win a championship. Those children wonder if they'll go their whole lives without seeing their team win and how much longer they have to sit in their wet diapers before someone notices.

Red Sox University supplies you with a wealth of information, some of it difficult to absorb at first. But our school is not all blood, sweat, and tears, nor is it earth, wind, and fire, nor Emerson, Lake & Palmer. It is meant to be fun. We encourage frequent trips to

RSU accepts students as young as six years of age.

the ballpark for extra credit, and every so often, if you're good, the city organizes a parade down the major streets of Back Bay connecting Fenway to the Commons and Government Center.

Throughout your education, you'll immerse yourself in Red Sox culture and the influence that the team has had on the city of Boston. Then you'll start to realize the immense reach that the Red Sox have, both geographically and chronologically, providing fans the most unique array of players that professional sports has ever seen. Many, though obscure, still maintain a place in the record books. Taking a brief look back, you'll see that there has been a Fabian, an Elston, a Bobo, a Nemo, a Chico, a Braggo, a Dropo, a Drago, a Walker, a Baker, a Gardner, a Speaker, and a Weaver. Candy, Sandy, Mandy, Pinky, Pokey, Tilly, Tubby, Dizzy,

Stuffy, Wiley, Windy, Bucky, Beany, Sparky, Skinny, and Slim played for Boston, too. Though they never did acquire Pee-Wee.

We had Hy and Lowe, Les and Moore, Far and Nomar, and Earley and Knight. Gray, White, Black, Brown, and Green (too bad they didn't get Vida Blue) have all worn red at one point or another. And so did Ski, Pinch, Pudge, Boomer, Hoot, Doc, Dud, Homer, Yank, Trot, Hick, Flash, Casper, Tex, Kip, Olaf, Clyde, and Ripley (believe it or not). Arquimedez, Hipolito, Ugie, and Coco called the Fens home for a while as well.

Bud and Lou, Amos and Andy, and Stan and Ollie all played for the Red Sox, as did Moe, Larry, and another Howard (Curly never made the cut). Neither did Jermaine, but they did sign Jackie, Tito, Marlan, and Michael.

Mike Myers, Jason, and Freddy played for Boston; they were all portrayed as psychos in the movies. Come to think of it, "Psycho" played for them, too.

Huey, Dewey, Luis, and Donald were members of Red Sox Nation. So was Mickey. And let's not forget about Rudy, Fergie, Iggy, Pumpsie, Heinie, Chappie, Monty, and Grady. Grady, by the way, was a rube, but Rube was not a grady.

Soup, Steamer, Camp, Horn, Snow, Wedge, Viola, Bell, Berry, Lake, Rice, Doerr, Winter, Mace, Bunk, Rose, and other inanimate nouns played for the team. No jokes please, but do you remember Dick Pole? (He wasn't related to Pesky's Pole.)

There were a Rabbit, a Bunny, a Birdie, a Gerbil, a Peacock, a Hawk, a Foxx, a Moose, a Monster, a Tartabull, some Buffalo Heads, a Trout, a Chick, and a Chicken Man all cooped inside that tiny clubhouse on Yawkey Way. A "Gentleman," a Parent, a "Papi," a "Kid," the "Gold Dust Twins," a "Spaceman," a Dean, a Judge, a Duke, a Lord, a Bishop, Jesus, Moses, and Angel all played for the same franchise that Israel did.

And as a testament to the historical impact the Boston Red Sox have had, they've fielded teams containing Hancock, Adams,

Van Buren, Jackson, Johnson, Taylor, Grover, Cleveland, Wilson, Ike, Kennedy, Johnson, Nixon, Regan, Bush, Clinton, and Bush.

That's just a small taste of the type of knowledge you'll acquire as a student at Red Sox University. So if you're ready, prepare to begin the most enjoyable and thorough education of your lives. Class is in session.

1

Biology

PREREQUISITE

You must have opposable thumbs.

LEARNING OBJECTIVES

After reading this chapter, you should be able to:

- Define each type of Red Sox fan
- Understand their DNA (Depressed Negative Attitude)
- Pinpoint key characteristics of each type
- Describe what each part of the Red Sox fan's brain does during a game
- Identify fans who look like Red Sox fans, but aren't

A Different Kind of Fan

Ribosomes, mitochondria, paramecium, and other biological terms—yes, Red Sox fans have them all, but why would we spend time discussing the commonalities between us and the rest of the world? For better or for worse, Sox fans are different. This first course at Red Sox University will discuss how the inherent personality of all Red Sox fans varies from the typical baseball fan's.

How could we and Pirates fans have sprung from the same loins of Adam? (Sorry, that's too creationist.) How could we have we evolved from the same beings? (Hmm, that's too liberal.) How do...bee do bee do? (Too Sinatra.) The question speaks to the subtleties that make us Red Sox fans and not, say, fans of the Marlins or Blue Jays. Is it just geographical? Or is it more than that?

The cause for our allegiance comes from deep within, perhaps from our genetic code. Noted biologist Dr. M. Memmem spent years crafting his thesis outlining what it's like to be a follower of the Boston baseball squad. Summarizing his findings, he quoted Jerry Maguire when describing the internal permutations of the Red Sox fan: "It is an up-at-dawn, pride-swallowing siege that I will never fully tell you about."

The Boston Brain

The brain of the Red Sox fan is not unlike that of the Yankees fan, except that the Sox fan's is more evolved. Also, it's four times larger and smells like peanut brittle, while a Yankees fan's brain smells of sulfur. But aside from that, they are quite similar. To use another analogy, compare a meal prepared by your three-year-old nephew and one prepared by Massachusetts native Emeril Lagasse. The elements are similar—the bowls, the spices, the notch-kicking, the cries of "Bam!"—but one's a heap of gruel while the other glows radiantly on the countertop crying out, "Hello! I invite you to eat me and have all your pleasures realized. Here is some tea with which to wash me down." [Note: after dumping all their tea in the Harbor more than two centuries ago, the only thing Bostonians have left to wash it down with is pomegranate juice.]

There is a misconception that the Red Sox fan only uses the right side or "emotional" part of his brain. In fact, there is a highly attuned left side that causes rational thought to prevail more often than not. But to truly understand the Boston brain, we must examine the type of stimuli that trigger emotional reactions inside a Red Sox fan's head. One commonly demonstrated trigger is the sight of pinstripes; when viewed by a Sox fan, the effect is not unlike the red cape of the toreador that provokes a bull's attack.

Say What?

"This is a must-win game."— to be used anytime the Sox have lost the previous game or are involved in a playoff series. It indicates you know the seriousness of the situation. If you're thinking the situation might not be serious, you aren't thinking rationally.

Consider the parable of the man at the wedding who, upon seeing pinstripes in the bride's father's suit, began ripping the father's clothes off. It was an awkward moment considering the father was in a chair being carried high above the crowd while the band played the Hora raucously. Cries of "Rabbi, no! Stop!" did little to squelch the confrontation. The moral of the story, obviously, is that one should not get married after the Yankees complete a three-game sweep of the Red Sox.

Analyzing the Cause

One must look deeper at the cause of such hidden rage, commonly referred to as **obstructed-view behavior.** It is characterized by the subject's visual field being limited to his or her periphery. In the case of the rabbi, his receptors blocked him from seeing the bridal party, the band, the wedding planner (though she was making out with the best man in the coat room at the time), the caterers, and the guests. He was focused only on the pinstripes. Even with his high-priced spectacles, it proves the point that even if you pay a lot of money, you can still get stuck with an obstructed view.

Our Personalities

As with any large group of people, you will find the personalities of Red Sox fans run the gamut. Some are emotional, some are *highly* emotional, while some spend their days beating on street lamps with a bat after tough losses. Still others make rationalizing and/or fretting about the most inconsequential decisions their favorite hobbies.

The brains of Red Sox fans can generally be divided into those with emotional centers, those with rational centers, and those with perception centers.

Emotional Centers

People with overactive emotional centers can experience the highest highs but are vulnerable to the lowest lows. And that's just during breakfast. A badly phrased remark can send them into a tailspin. What may seem harmless to some sends them teetering toward the precipice of finality. (Pretty deep, huh?)

Consider this example of an emotional fan's reaction to an innocent statement:

> *Radio talk-show host:* "Lester's pitching great,
> Ortiz is on a hot streak, Youk's back..."
> *Emotional fan:* "What?! What's wrong with
> Youk's back?!" [Reaches for bedside cyanide pills]

The proper way to phrase that statement is, "Kevin Youkilis has returned from an injury." Do not allow emotional fans any

KEY TERMS

obstructed-view behavior—a behavioral pattern that causes one to narrow his or her focus to only Red Sox–related news

opportunity to misconstrue your words. Though it's not your fault, the emotional brain centers translate information differently and more swiftly than do rational centers.

The insufficient release of serotonin is often the cause of these inappropriate reactions. This neurotransmitter is like the "Hey Jude" of the brain—it takes a sad song and makes it better. Not enough serotonin and that song will never be better.

Emotional types have been seen around Fenway making snap decisions, whether it's throwing pizza at another fan or taking a swing at a visiting right fielder in an effort to scoop up the ball. A rational fan would make a more reasonable assessment and determine if the ball was in play, if an interjection would help or hurt the team, and, mainly, if it's legal—all within a split second. Chicago Cubs scapegoat and foul-ball enthusiast Steve Bartman is of the emotional persuasion.

Rational Centers

Imagine an early June series with the Yankees that sees New York take two out of three and increase their lead in the AL East to a seemingly insurmountable four games. Whereas those with dominant emotional centers are making reservations on the Zakim Bridge, fans with dominant rational centers realize that Josh Beckett did not pitch, the previous day's rain caused a slicker ball to sneak under Dustin Pedroia's glove, and a guy in the third row behind home plate wore a gold chain that reflected a flare into Jonathan Papelbon's eye at the wrong moment.

To a rational fan, all of these events are coincidental and a knowledge of baseball history shows that you can't win them all. They would argue that one series does not dictate the outcome of another, and that one series in June has little bearing on whether or not the Yankees are the better team.

Art of the Pizza Toss

When tossing a slice of pizza at a fellow Sox fan,
always follow these instructions:

GO BACK TO
GREEN BAY
YA CHEESEHEADS!

1	Hold the slice of pizza with the pointy side between your index and middle fingers. (Exception: if the slice is from somewhere other than Papa Gino's, you can toss it like a Frisbee.)
2	Stand up first. The seats at Fenway are too close together to throw from your butt. Create some space by standing on top of your seat if necessary.
3	Wait until the cameras are on you. It doesn't count if no one but your section knows you're the culprit.
4	Toss the pizza like a shot put, making sure to achieve only a one-half rotation. In other words, the cheese should begin toward the sky and land facedown on the victim's clothing.
5	Point at your target and laugh. This is also the best time to make some lame jokes, such as: "Go back to Green Bay, ya cheesehead!" "Hey, everyone! Pizza's on him!" "Delivered to your face in 30 minutes or less!"
6	Wave to the crowd as security yanks you out of your seat by the hair and escorts you from the ballpark.

However, rational fans of the Red Sox are still predisposed to slipping into emotional thought patterns compared to rational fans of other big-league teams.

Say the front office has told the manager his star pitcher is on a 100-pitch count limit. Let's also assume the manager has a bullpen that is almost perfect in the playoffs and that he's facing a lineup that thrives on seeing a starter more than twice in a game. Finally, let's imagine the opponent is your hated **rival** that has beaten you, oh, let's just use a number at random here, 85 of the last 85 years. Should this hypothetical manager maintain stubbornness with said pitcher and allow a lead to disintegrate, it causes rational thought to give way to emotion. This is natural. It is frustration caused by the inability to do anything to personally rectify the situation.

But unlike their emotional counterparts, the rational fan will not take their hand and smash it through a plate glass window. That would do damage to their body while doing nothing to alleviate the situation. More likely, they will take someone else's hand and smash it through a plate glass window. They might also consider tipping over a chest-high bar table with pitchers of beer and plates of wings and blue cheese on it, thus creating a mess but causing no physical harm. Using common sense in moments

KEY TERMS

rivals [ri'valz] *n*—two teams that play each other frequently and constantly rag on the other's city and fans—*n* **rivalry**, a verbal battle where one side constantly brings up things that happened ages ago and the second wishes the first side be destroyed in a vat of their own comeuppance

of stress is where rational fans differentiate themselves from emotional fans.

There are still questions pertaining to the value of cold, disassociated thinking. For example, fans with rational brains plan terrible parades. The rational thought pattern also presents a difficult proposition for talent evaluators. Consider a player who has great numbers but remains lifeless as a clubhouse presence, then experiences a numbers slide during crucial moments (i.e., disappears in the playoffs). Should he remain on the team?

Perception Centers

A third type of Boston brain pattern further differentiates its biology from the brains of other fans. Let's look at it this way—a normal brain gathers information from multiple senses and then acts based upon a reasoned analysis of the data. But to a brain that relies completely on its perception center, all actions and beliefs are based directly on one's *perception* of reality; any other information is immaterial. Whereas most fans can read the news or financial section of the newspaper without thinking of their favorite team, a Boston fan with an overactive perception center thinks everything involves the Red Sox. Put another way, a normal fan sees an entire spectrum of colors; a Boston fan sees only red.

Actual Morning Headline	What a Red Sox Fan Sees
"Stocks Continue to Plummet"	"Lineup Stricken by Slump"
"Killer Still at Large"	"Sox Fall Further Behind Yankees"
"Babies Spontaneously Combust, Scientists Baffled"	"Bullpen Implodes Again, Manager Sticks with Closer"

The behavior of those with perception-centered brains is often unpredictable; they can take either emotional or rational actions. Most of the time, all three types of brains are influenced by the specific class a fan belongs to. As with breeds of dogs, we are not all born of the same litter.

Say What?

"Go Sox!"—this is said in passing to other Red Sox fans. "Go Sox!" is the equivalent to "What's up?" or "Hey" when entering the same space as someone else.

A Class Study

To further understand the biological construction of a Red Sox fan, we must discuss the classifications that distinguish between types of Red Sox fans. As a whole, Red Sox fans are part of the sports family *Passionatsia* and belong to the order *wicked fanatica* and the class *Bostonia*. The scientific name of their kingdom is *freakin' pissah*. (They are never to be confused with a Yankees fan's kingdom, the *brutus droolifica*.)

As you look around Fenway and throughout the Nation, the untrained eye can highlight the similarities that identify someone as a Red Sox fan—the same hats, the same Ortiz jersey, the same cars blaring their horns at you even though you have the light, etc. We want you to focus on what's *different* when comparing Red Sox fans. Through several "double-blind, L-fly button-hook pattern, snap-on-two" studies here at the University, we have classified 12 different types of Red Sox fans.

Idiots

Overview

A fun-loving, ragtag group of fans, they are technically the first generation to have shaken the culture of losing…and chose to embrace the culture of drinking. Their ages run the gamut, all the way from those in their early twenties to those in their late early twenties. (Or at least that's how old they behave.) They have prominent Southie accents, but only because they've seen *Good Will Hunting* more than 100 times. Their first names are unknown even to one another, as they refer to each other only by some variant of their last names.

Fisticuffs is a dialect many of them speak. Hugging them is not recommended, regardless of the score of the game in progress.

Where You Can Find Them	In the bleachers or at one of the bars along Brookline Avenue. The latter location gives them easy access to cars in Kenmore Square for tipping should something important or momentous happen. Like wolves, Idiots usually travel in packs. Wherever they are, one of them will start a chant such as "Let's Go, Red Sox! [clap clap clapclapclap]" and the rest of the pack will soon join in. Eventually one of them will change the words to something like "I am hun-gry! [clap clap clapclapclap]"
Pregame Preparation	Idiots get fired up before a game by walking down the street scaring pedestrians by aggressively seeking high fives. It's a good thing if you're on their side, but that might not matter should they be especially high-spirited.
Game Attire	Something easily removable and possibly offensive to the masses. Popular options include T-shirts with phrases like "Jeter eats ****" or "The Yankees are a bunch of ******" or "Posada **** his mother's ***** ****** while ****** a rotten ******." (That last one often runs onto the back of the shirts.) If they're not wearing a shirt, they have most likely painted something on their chests… and misspelled it.
Secret Desire	To run on the field high-fiving the players while being cheered by their fellow fans. The only thing stopping them on most evenings is they're too drunk to get that first foot over the railing without stumbling and falling back into their seats.

GMs (General Managers)

Overview

These are the radio talk-show regulars. What do they do all day? They call in to complain about the Red Sox. What do they do with their spare time? They think of things to say when they call in to complain about the Red Sox. They believe they would make better general managers than Theo Epstein and proceed to offer up inane trades, such as:

"Look, this is perfect: Boston should do a three-team deal where we get Albert Pujols from

St. Louis and we send the rights to Bruce Hurst—should he ever decide to come out of retirement—to Toronto, and then Toronto sends us Roy Halladay. Then we can send a couple of minor leaguers to St. Louis if they whine about it not being a fair deal."

Overview, continued

One sure-fire way to identify a GM is to pay attention to the way his call ends; if the host disconnects him or plays the "explosion" sound effect, the caller was definitely a GM.

GMs should not be confused with "first-time, long-time" callers. However, if you hear someone call a show and say they're a "first-time *listener*, long-time *caller*," they should automatically be reclassified as a GM.

Disposition	GMs are usually unhappy with the way things are going and with the way the team has been put together, and they cannot understand why the real-life GM is such a festering boil on the side of a sweaty boar.
Background	They have several fantasy teams and very little social interaction with people who care about what they think, which makes them uniquely qualified to call talk shows and annoy the listening audience.
Dream Job	Talk-radio host, general manager of a sports team, Red Sox Nation president, Unabomber, or high school janitor.
Game Habits	GMs complain before, during, and after the game, and also about any play that does not go Boston's way. Most likely, they are currently complaining about everything in this book. In fact, they're probably calling WEEI right this minute to complain about it.

Dirt Dogs

Overview

These guys are good examples of what we, as a Nation, are striving for—selfless, true-blue fans. Dirt Dogs live in the trenches and don't come out. They do whatever they can to help the Red Sox win. You may be thinking to yourself, *What can fans possibly do to help the Red Sox win?* Oh, do you have a lot to learn.

They'll sacrifice one for the team. If the Sox win on a night the Dirt Dog was sick, he'll keep his cold until their winning streak is over. Or he'll find another cold. Either way, he's getting germs to help the team win.

They also take losses very personally. Dirt Dogs feel there was always something they could've done to root just a little bit harder. But they don't shy away from blame. Some might even hold a press conference to apologize to their fellow fans for waxing optimistic about the possibility of consecutive championships in a premature fashion.

Duties

A Dirt Dog will keep track of the outs for everyone around them. After a double play, he'll put up two fingers and explain, "Okay, two away. We need one more, people. Let's bear down here." He tells his friends to sit in the appropriate seats, positions, or formation. He knows the right chant and when to start it. He's there through thick and thin and will hunker down to watch the play when others (see: Ostriches) cover their eyes and look away.

Attitude

They are the most humble of all Red Sox fans. When someone compliments them for their efforts after the game, they're likely to say, "There were hundreds of us out there doing the same thing I was. It's a team effort. I just want to win. I play my role so others can play theirs."

Favorite Pastime

Waiting for the other shoe to fall. Five outs remaining? That's nothing. One out? Child's play. The fates are just warming up.

They know the history of the team as well as anyone. Dirt Dogs know it's not over until the late-night talk-show hosts start having Sox players on as guests. They keep the champagne well hidden, and they don't want to know that championship shirts have been printed, and for the love of all that is holy, don't even *think* about planning the parade route. Dogs do not officially stop worrying until the final out is recorded. Only then do they celebrate.

Ostriches

Overview

Named after one of nature's most valiant creatures, these protectors of the meek typically…oh, who are we kidding? They're essentially chickens. Ostriches are the opposite of Dirt Dogs, but it does not make them bad fans. Like the animal, they tend to bury their heads in the sand, figuratively speaking, when the going gets tough.

However, do not be fooled by their apparent disappearance during tense game moments. Ostriches may actually be the most loyal of all fans; they disappear only because they believe it allows the team to triumph. Many Ostriches won't watch the game live, but will watch the highlights immediately after it's over. It's much less stressful that way.

Behavior	Ostriches believe good things won't happen if they are there to see them, and there is anecdotal evidence to support their theory. An Ostrich will miss a Clay Buchholz no-hitter, but will tune in to see the kid shelled for six runs in one-third of an inning. It's eerie how it works out that way. Hence, they insist on going to the bathroom, walking around the house, starting a jigsaw puzzle, or anything else that keeps their attention off the game and prevents bad luck from afflicting the team.
Transformation Process	Ostriches often resemble other fans at the outset of a game —affable, comfortable in their seats, and anxious to watch the events unfold. Then the Red Sox give up a base hit, perhaps a blooper. A walk follows. It is then that an Ostrich's stomach starts to flutter; he or she will squirm uncontrollably in their seats. Frenetically, they begin to look for an escape to the nearest exit or the bathroom. Their throats dry, and they lurch from their comfy perch to prevent seeing anything further. If they are actually at the game, they bump into vendors as they rush up the aisles toward the out-of-view concourse. If they are at home, they quickly excuse themselves and watch something more tranquil, like *The Texas Chain Saw Massacre*.
Psychology	Most of them are past their twenties and have been traumatized by the Red Sox for most of their lives. Imagine witnessing your father run over your dog. From that day forward, you cringe every time you see your father behind the wheel of a car. Similarly, Ostriches have been conditioned to expect the worst. "It hasn't happened if you don't watch it happen" is their motto. What difference does it make if you watch the events or not, just as long as it ends well? You can certainly watch the parade. Nothing bad can happen there, right?

Pink Hats

Overview

These are the newest arrivals to the Nation; they existed before 2004, but have multiplied exponentially since then. They believe that all the games end with a reality dating show, such as *Sox Appeal*. They are the most maligned and probably the most noticeable, but did you know that they often don't actually wear pink clothing? Pink Hats are the cause of most of the dissension in Red Sox Nation.

Origins	The term comes from the recent fad of pink-colored clothing, usually marketed to women but proudly worn by men one week in 2004 when the *Queer Eye for the Straight Guy* crew made over the previously macho Johnny Damon, Tim Wakefield, Jason Varitek, Doug Mirabelli, and Kevin Millar.
Behavior	Pink Hats attempt to blend into the scenery and usually will not participate in any chant for fear that they will embarrass themselves. It's like being in church and trying to sing along with a hymn you've never heard before, so you just mumble a little bit and make it look like you're singing. If they are part of a couple, they spend time holding hands or even snuggling, as they might do in a movie theatre. That's a no-no.
Tell-Tale Signs	At first, they seem to fit in, but eventually they will slip up and you'll realize who they are. David Ortiz's nickname is pronounced "Big Poppy," not "Big Pappy." It is Jonathan *Papelbon*, not Jonathan *Papelbaum*. (He's not Jewish.) Often, a Pink Hat will ask "Why are they booing Youk?" without realizing the crowd is saying "Youuuuuuuuuk!" Once you have identified a Pink Hat , you can handle them one of two ways: take a deep breath, smile, and calmly clarify things for them before an Idiot does it in a more aggressive manner, or explain to them that league rules stipulate they are not allowed back inside a major league ballpark until they learn the players' names and the cheers that accompany them. Since they're not too familiar with baseball, they'll believe you, at least for a while.
Attire	Crisp, new merchandise, without creases, stains, smudges, or blemishes. A Dirt Dog must resist the urge to grab their caps and stomp on them just to add some authenticity.

Late Bloomers

Overview

Baseball is a long season and these fans don't bother coming to Fenway during the dog days of summer. They'll come into bloom, so to speak, around August or September. Fair-weather fans? Perhaps on the surface, but win or lose, Late Bloomers are there for the team's two good months per year. They're like September call-ups; an infusion of fresh fans is often just what's needed when you're headed down the stretch.

Habits	Late Bloomers skip the appetizers and go right to the main course. They read the news on the monitor in the elevator at work. They change the radio station with the buttons on the steering wheel of their cars, instead of reaching a whole six inches to the console. They use shampoo and conditioner in the same bottle. They can't be bothered with things that take time. They'll keep informed of the team with to-the-point questions like, "Sox got a shot this year?" and "Are the Yanks still in it?" It affords them the time to get their work done before they start altering their sleep patterns to follow the team in autumn.
Tendencies	Given to changing the subject whenever baseball comes up early in the season, they tend to be masters of many subjects, which keeps them occupied until crunch time. Taxes are a popular topic through April and early May, then barbecuing tips for Memorial Day, their summer plans through June, advice on dealing with the humidity in July and August, and then—*boom!*—they're ready for baseball season. Right on time.

Ask the Valedictorian

When is it okay to call your friends to celebrate a victory?

Treat a celebratory phone call like a radio contest: be the first caller after you hear the magic song. If you call before the song, you lose.

Similarly, an early phone call to a friend will cause the team to lose. You may remember the scoreboard operators at Shea Stadium congratulating the "1986 World Champion Boston Red Sox" before Calvin Schiraldi imploded. We all know how that turned out.

Calling friends who are fans of different teams and trying to jinx them tends to backfire, and also opens you up to them doing it to you. It's one of those unwritten rules of fandom, similar to players not slapping a ball out of an opponent's glove or yelling "I got it!" as they run the base paths to distract an infielder. We leave those kinds of bush-league antics to bad baseball fans and Alex Rodriguez.

Mirabelles

Overview	ESPN.com's Bill Simmons once referred to female fans of the Red Sox as being built like Doug Mirabelli. (If you don't know who Doug is, you are either a Pink Hat or a Late Bloomer.) Mirabelles are broad-shouldered women who wear their hats backward to hide their long hair, so it's understandable that they might be mistaken for Tim Wakefield's personal catcher for many years. They wear authentic Red Sox jerseys, devoid of any pink or non-team colors, have a beer in each hand, and possess a vocabulary that would make Tito Francona blush.
Baseball IQ	Through the roof: they know who's up, what he's batting, his shoe size, which bar he likes to frequent after games, and any other pertinent information.
Weaknesses	Walking a straight line after the game, remembering where they parked, the letter "R."

Oh, Really?

A typical trip from Logan Airport to Fenway Park during rush hour averages 58 minutes. Add 240 pounds in the form of one-time catcher Doug Mirabelli and the trip drops to 12 minutes.

KEY TERMS

American League Championship Series
[ay ell see ess] *n*—a best-of-seven playoff series in October to determine who will represent the American League in the World Series, it can only be won once you are down three games to one or none

Tekkies

Overview	They wear more pink than the Pink Hats; after all, they want to look their best for Varitek, Papelbon, Pedroia, Ellsbury, or anyone else that wears the uniform. But remember, simply wearing pink does not a Pink Hat make.
Marital Status	They are married, though only in their imaginations. A Tekkie will refer to her favorite player as "my husband." "Oh, they hit it to my husband." "How did my husband play today?" "My husband has the nicest butt on the team." Note that a Tekkie's "husband" changes weekly. One week it's Varitek, another it's Papelbon, then in a rather saucy fantasy ménage, it's Pedroia *and* Ellsbury. Unfortunately, their desire knows no allegiance. Tekkies even think Derek Jeter looks cute. Ewwwwwww.

Attire	Tekkies favor replica jerseys just like Mirabelles do, but the similarities end there. With a Red Sox hat in place and their ponytails coming out the back, Tekkies keep their jerseys unbuttoned to reveal adorable tank-tops underneath, often ones featuring a phrase like, "Real Women Don't Date Yankees Fans." Then they apply the requisite sunblock, sparkly lip gloss, and top it off with some bold Dolce & Gabbana sunglasses.
Beverage of Choice	A cup of light beer, followed by two bottles of water to stay hydrated. Tekkies are always prepared to finally meet their "husband" after the game and they need their skin to be at its best.
Knowledge	Mirabelles are miles ahead of Tekkies in terms of baseball IQ. When you speak to Tekkies about a player's "makeup," be prepared to get into a long discussion about how they should use plenty of foundation before applying anything too bold.

KEY TERMS

no more *adj*—used to quantify a change in traditions such as "the Curse of the Bambino" or the Yankees' dominance (e.g., the Yankees are better than us no more)

POP QUIZ

Q How many wins did brothers Pedro and Ramon Martinez combine for in 1999?

A 25, thanks largely to Ramon's two wins.

Royal Rooters

Overview

Named for the most famous fan club in the country and our ancestral founders, we owe a lot to them. Although some of them are no longer with us, their spirit lives on in anyone who has passed the half-century mark as a Red Sox fan.

Male or female, Royal Rooters comprise the senior circuit of Red Sox Nation. They may not know who the left-handed set-up man du jour is, but they also don't think it makes sense to give a roster spot to someone who only pitches to one batter. They watched guys throw until their arms fell off and then they watched as the manager let them pitch to two more batters. (Upon going to the showers, the starter would always doff his cap to the crowd with his one remaining arm.)

Philosophy	Royal Rooters long for the days before free agency and revenue sharing. There was no interleague play or DH back in "the day." The game had integrity. No one was shooting up and increasing their hat sizes along with their home-run totals. They were playing their hearts out for very little money because they loved the game…while on a steady diet of greenies and uppers to keep them focused. Now that was baseball!
Knowledge	They don't lend themselves to Tim McCarvian points of hyperbole such as, "He's probably the greatest left-handed pinch-hitter to ever lace up his cleats." Rooters can tell you of at least four better left-handed pinch-hitters, because they've seem them all play.
Behavior	Royal Rooters love to keep score during the game. There's an old tale about a Rooter who was sitting next to a Pink Hat. The first batter hits a fly ball to the center fielder, who makes a nice running catch. The Rooter says, "Score that play an '8,'" and writes it down. The next batter hits it directly to the right fielder. The Rooter says "Score that play a '9,'" at which point the Pink Hat leans over to him and says, "I thought the first catch was better." (If you didn't understand that story, you're probably a Pink Hat.)

POP QUIZ

Q Is Jimmy Fallon a Red Sox fan?

A No.

Touristas

Overview	Touristas may root for Boston, but they are not citizens of Red Sox Nation. While they might be Red Sox fans, they're a much different type of fan.

When They Come Out	If the Red Sox are in their town and the team is good, a Tourista might try to purchase a couple of tickets to impress a significant other. (Besides, Springsteen won't be in town for another three weeks and they've got to find something to do to keep them from talking about "our relationship.")
Game Behavior	Wearing crisp, brand-new hats and shirts sans creases or stains, Touristas sit in their seats and focus on the game as if they know what's going on. They'll try to engage their fellow fans, but should really just keep their mouths shut. "Who's on the mound?" doesn't really endear you to other fans when it's Tim Wakefield, the pitcher who is third on the team's all-time wins list.
Where to Find Them	In ballparks and bars far from Fenway Park. Not all Red Sox fans living in other cities are Touristas; some of the world's finest Sox fans are forced to live outside of Massachusetts. Also, if someone in Fenway appears to be acting like a Tourista, they are most likely a Pink Hat.
Translation	In English, they are simply a *tourist,* which is how George W. Bush pronounces the word *terrorist.* Rest assured, these fans are not dangerous. But it's possible that they know less about baseball than fundamentalist extremists do.
Blohards (a subset of Touristas)	These are members of the Benevolent Loyal Order of the Honorable Ancient Red Sox Die-Hard Sufferers of New York. They don't mess around. They are hardened from living in the belly of the beast, also known as New York City. Nothing fazes them. They have proven themselves by passing the tests of courage, spirit, fire (many Yankees fans grab their hats and light them on fire), and loyalty. Many have the New York accent, the New York mindset, but the Boston personality. That is to say, they are not as likely to throw a hot dog with mustard at your face. These fans are very knowledgeable.

Rising Sons

Overview	These are Japanese fans of our Japanese players.
Motive	They are not as much interested in the Boston Red Sox as they are in our Far East imports. They follow Dice-K and whatever he does. When he doesn't pitch, they want to know what he had for breakfast, or, as they call it in Japan, "breakfast." (They speak a lot of English in Japan.)
Accessories	They have a camera surgically attached to their necks and a Japanese-to-English dictionary on their persons at all times. Though they tend to speak differently than Bostonians, there are times when they are easier to understand than Bostonians.

Fenway Japanese

Be a good host. Take some time to teach a Rising Son some popular English phrases. Here are some helpful sayings with which to start them off:

1. Swing and a drive…Way back!…Way back!
2. Papelbon is lights out.
3. A-Rod is a cheater.
4. Papi! Papi! Papi!
5. Did you read Shaughnessy's column last night?
6. "The Big Show with the Big O"
7. Yes, but how many championships have they won this century?
8. I miss Trot.
9. Why is Tito leaving him in so long?

Side Effects

WARNING: Being a Red Sox fan might cause anxiety, shortness of breath, nausea, the shakes, dry mouth, dry heaves, ringing in the ears, rabid heartbeat, palpitations, vomiting, blurred vision, hyperventilation, gastrointestinal trouble, uncontrollable sobbing, mood swings, depression, euphoria, ennui, a boycott of Japan, a desire for more, fear, anger, frustration, sadness, humility, love, hate, everything in between, rudeness, insanity, paralysis, a need for a hug, vertigo, a loss of class, a farewell to grace, a call to arms, extended periods of mourning, morning sickness, coated tongue, swollen glands, inflamed joints, joint stiffness, osteoporosis, alcoholism, shock, dismay, futility, a resemblance to Chicken Little, bruised ego, loss of appendix, the desire to shout "Woo!" during private ceremonies, pugilism, loneliness, silliness, yelling at inanimate objects, the Cuban Missile Crisis, the Big Dig, Joanie loving Chachi, appearing in a tank with a helmet three sizes too large, shouting "There's only one October!" on television, impotency, lewd behavior, sudden attack by hawks, a frayed O-ring in the space shuttle, incorrect horoscopes, insomnia, weak bladder, heart arrhythmia, and, in rare cases, death.

Ben Afflecks

Overview	This subset of Red Sox Nation isn't particularly abundant, but can be seen almost everywhere.
Hobbies	Flying in from out of town to take in a Sox game, trying to one-up Matt Damon, having children with Jennifer Garner, goofing around with Jimmy Kimmel, periodically working on his abs, being politically active, and directing his brother in movies.
Appearance	He's not the quintessential Red Sox fan, considering he was once named "Sexiest Man Alive" in *People* magazine. Most Sox fans would be lucky to get honorable mention in the "Guys Who Remember to Leave the Seat Down" article in *Real-Life Monthly*.
Wannabes	There are many who strive to be Ben Afflecks—Matt Damon, Mark Wahlberg, Dane "There's only one October!" Cook, and Senator John Kerry, to name a few—but they pale in comparison.

Summary

The study of Red Sox biology is not easy and requires a discerning eye. Although ideologically identical, slight variations in thought processes, behavior, or speech patterns produce a broad spectrum of fans. They might be striving for the same goals, but many are at odds over the ways and means...just like Democrats.

Fun at the Park

Attend a Red Sox game. Clearly identify eight different breeds of Red Sox fans. What distinguishes them as such?

1.

2.

3.

4.

5.

6.

7.

8.

Test Your Knowledge

How are *Pink Hats* and *Touristas* different? Next to whom would you rather sit at a Red Sox game?

What would cause you to throw a slice of pizza? To interfere with an opposing outfielder?

Which type of fan are you? Which characteristics make you that way?

Fist bump or high five—which is your celebratory gesture of choice?

Matching Test

Match the fans with one of their defining characteristics.

____ 1. Pink Hats

____ 2. Dirt Dogs

____ 3. Touristas

____ 4. Tekkies

____ 5. Ostriches

____ 6. Ben Afflecks

____ 7. Late Bloomers

____ 8. Mirabelles

____ 9. Idiots

____ 10. GMs

A. plot to eliminate the real wives of the players

B. resemble the enemy but are on our side

C. can block the plate as well as anyone

D. have easy access to Matt Damon

E. look at the All-Star Game as spring training

F. want to trade all our young talent for the reigning Cy Young winner

G. think throwing beer bottles at the riot police is funny

H. are surprised to learn that "stealing" is legal

I. spend a lot of time in the bathroom

J. apologize for ruining a no-hitter

2

History

There's no point learning about the present without having an appreciation of the past, a sense of history, and a love of a good story. How did we, as a Nation, get to this point? Our forefathers did a lot to mold us; some were more benevolent than others, but whether unbeknownst to you or knownst to you, they all had a hand in our evolution as fans.

Most of the Nation's growth as citizens and as fans came after moments of great adversity. We relive four of those periods here.

Competition for Attention

The spring of 1901 came early. The rain was fresh, flowers bloomed, a city's spirit was renewed, and a new baseball season brought with it a different feeling that spread throughout the city.

For fans accustomed to watching the National League's Boston Braves, 1901 marked the first time Bostonians were given a choice between two local baseball teams, thanks to the new Boston Americans.

The Americans had been led to roost by the commissioner of the new American League, Ban Johnson. That's why they were unofficially dubbed the "Americans," though some people called them the "Pilgrims," the "Red Stockings," and most popularly, "the Boston team, aside from that *other* Boston team."

Though they garnered some interest at first, they still had competition from their crosstown rivals. It wasn't until 1903 that the junior-circuit club began to seize on the attentions of the loyal denizens, plucking them from the local taverns and placing them into the stands of Huntington Avenue Grounds.

Success Comes to Boston

The American Red Stockinged Pilgrims were winning. At the same time, fans around town had a collective epiphany—they liked winning. In fact, they couldn't get enough of it. They had to have more. Boston's new squad now had a fan base.

The National League quickly became jealous of their baby siblings and conspired against them. They offered a chance to battle for supremacy in a series that would determine the champion of the world. They would call it the "Series to Determine the Champion of the World" or the "STDTCOTW" for short.

The young, upstart league with their young, upstart franchise accepted the challenge, but little did they know what was in store for them.

The First World Series

Pittsburgh represented the National League and on the afternoon of October 1, 1903, the Pirates ambushed the Americans in front of more than 16,000 fans, leaving them shocked and humiliated in what later became known as "Game 1."

Eventually finding themselves down three games to one, things looked grim for Boston's manager/third baseman/regional sales director Jimmy Collins. Pittsburgh was doing exactly what they had set out to do. But Collins had other plans.

At the time of the first World Series, baseball was played with more outfielders than are used today.

He reached down deep before Game 5 and gave his team a pep talk they would not soon forget. He called them together in the locker room and stared at his troops for 30 minutes. He looked at the fear in their eyes and could see the doubt in their hearts. And with their full attention, he raised one finger into the air and barked so that each and every teammate could hear him: "Win!"

And they did. Four games in a row to win the first ever Series to Determine the Champion of the World.

Trophy After Trophy

Over the next 15 years, the scenario repeated itself four more times as Boston's newest team became Boston's newest sweetheart (though manly sweethearts at that). It happened so often that they decided to give the team a permanent name—the Red Sox. This prosperity continued until one of their own players turned on them and cursed the franchise in an act of vengeance and voodoo magic.

A Fall From Grace

The year was 1919, and George Ruth (a player named after both his father and his mother) was becoming an unruly citizen with his drinking and womanizing and, quite frankly, a case of the wind like you wouldn't believe. And though he had helped to win multiple championships and had just set the single-season mark for home runs, he was deemed expendable.

The owner of the Red Sox at the time, Harry Frazee, used his players as trading chips in order to raise money for his Broadway productions. He'd already found a fitting partner for his dealings in the owner of the New York Yankees; Frazee liked money and the Yankees had money to spend.

Upon being informed of the trade on December 26, 1919, a drunken Ruth stumbled through the clubhouse to retrieve his belongings, then turned back to reporters and bellowed, "You'll all be sorry! I put a curse on you that will last almost nine decades. You'll see. Say good-bye to success!" And then he gathered up his pet Pomeranian, Success, and made for the door, never to be heard from again (well, we heard from him a little).

With the money Frazee made from that and future deals, he was occasionally forced to field teams consisting entirely of stacks of cash. He'd put $15,000 in right field, a couple grand at shortstop, and a wad of singles at first. Needless to say, they didn't do very well.

The Age of Prosperity had officially ended.

The Great Uprising of 1967

For many years, the Red Sox languished in the gutter of the American League, like winos in the sport of life. Eight straight campaigns had ended in failure, with the team unable to win half their games in any of them, once finishing with 100 losses, the breaking point for most fans.

The city had lost all sense of self-respect and hope. Bostonians flocked from the ballpark in droves, turning their favors over to such alternate diversions as Cape Cod or Symphony Hall. Yes, times had sunk *that* low.

KEY TERMS

"The Curse of the Bambino" [bup'kiss] *n*— a curse placed on the team by former Red Sox player Babe Ruth upon being traded to the Yankees for cash and two boxes of Dunkin' Donuts

Episode IV: A New Hope

Captain Carl Yastrzemski knelt aside his locker, wondering what would become of his team this year and how so much lint could accumulate in one man's belly button. Suddenly, he heard a voice from behind him, gruff in timber, even gruffer in demeanor. The pointed tone behind it made Yaz sit up and take notice. It was his new manager, Dick Williams, who informed the team there was a new sheriff in town.

In an animated manner, Williams began to call everyone out, pointing around the clubhouse. "You, Jim Lonborg," he said to his star pitcher, "I'm going to need a Cy Young performance from you this year." He swiveled, "And you, Captain," he said with less reverence than sarcasm in the word. "I want you to lead the league in hits, homers, and RBIs just like Frank Robinson did last year." And with that, Williams pounded a dent into an unclaimed locker.

Oh, Really?

Although he attended USC on a scholarship, Red Sox center fielder Fred Lynn was so poor in college that he had to share a name with his roommate, future Steelers wide receiver Lynn Swann. (They stole it from major league pitcher Lynn Ryan, who went by his middle name, Nolan.) Fred went on to win the AL Rookie of the Year and the MVP Awards in 1975. Eventually, he earned enough money to pay Swann for sole use of the name (except on Sundays when the Steelers were playing).

Then, standing on a stool in the middle of the room, he addressed the rest of the congregants who looked at him in awe and fear. "As for the rest of you, I'm going to need an all-out effort from you! That's 162 games and not one less. Or else we ain't going nowhere! I ask 100 percent from all of you or you're not worthy to be on my team! No one rests until we've won the pennant!" And with that, Williams walked into his office and took a nap while the team played their first game of the year.

Doing the Impossible

Opening Day 1967 saw only 8,324 fans, and that number included the rats living in the left-field scoreboard. But as the season went on, the team refused to fade. Word spread throughout the town. From Symphony Hall to the Cape, fans began to return to the Fens, wearing caps reclaimed from the attic. The Great Uprising had begun.

FENWAY FACTS

Cy Young never won the Cy Young Award, but he did win Mr. Congeniality twice.

Fans witnessed each of Williams' charges doing exactly as he asked of them. And by September, the Red Sox were in unfamiliar territory—first place. But they weren't alone, as Chicago, Minnesota, and Detroit all laid claim to the throne. One-half game separated the four teams for most of that month.

The grueling fight dragged through the sweat-soaked late summer and into the autumn. The White Sox decided to bow out of the race in order to focus on more pressing matters, such as choosing original Halloween costumes. That left three teams vying for one spot. The Tigers, who would be heading to California, were tied with Boston; the Twins, who would be coming to Fenway, were one game ahead.

But destiny was not entirely in Boston's hands. The Fates held some of the cards. In order for their improbable march to continue, several things had to happen: the Detroit Tigers would have to lose one more game, the Chicago White Sox would have to stay eliminated, the first African American justice would have to be sworn into the Supreme Court, and the Red Sox would have to sweep Minnesota.

The disparity in the number of spectators between the first game of the year and these, the last ones, was reflective of the team's resurrection. Fans hung on every pitch as they watched

Williams, who had by now joined his team in the dugout, wring each last ounce of greatness from his players. The Red Sox won both games, completing the sweep and overtaking the Twins.

The players returned to the clubhouse to await their future. With Thurgood Marshall's appointment inevitable, the only thing they needed was an Angels victory over the Tigers. Mike Andrews sat glued to the radio while the rest of the team laughed at him for falling for one of the world's oldest practical jokes.

As Rico Petrocelli retrieved some turpentine to help his double-play partner unglue himself and avoid any further embarrassment, word came that the Tigers had lost. Boston had risen from ninth place to first place, thus fulfilling the wishes of their manager, who had much earlier left the park and headed for a local bar.

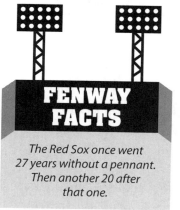

FENWAY FACTS

The Red Sox once went 27 years without a pennant. Then another 20 after that one.

Though they lost to a buzz-killing St. Louis Cardinals squad, the spirit and dedication of that one 1967 Boston Red Sox team spoke to the fans and did more for the city than Peter Faneuil ever did. Seriously, what did Boston need with more shops? And those cobblestones are murder on the feet.

One might think that a story like that was impossible, or that it could only be conjured in a dream. And maybe it was, but it was that unlikely season that rebuilt a Nation of fans and hastened the city of Boston into a golden age of almost-winning baseball.

The Fall of 1978

In 1948, Sox fans lived with a blissful exuberance. The war had ended and the Baby Boom had begun. Most Bostonians had no idea of the horror that would take place a mere 30 years later.

Ask the Valedictorian

Is it okay to cry?

Former player and women's baseball league manager Jimmy Dugan said it best when he said, "There's no crying in baseball." He also said to "avoid the clap," but that doesn't pertain to baseball as much as it does one's social life.

But if you absolutely *must* cry, be sure to cover your face with a towel, even if the screams of anguish become so shrill that they drive hyenas away in fear. If you do not have a towel, use the person next to you.

On the other hand, crying for joy is different and can be done on your own or with champagne stinging your retinas like tear gas, just as long as your team has been victorious moments earlier. One exception is remembering Dave Roberts' steal of third or Keith Foulke's toss to first base. Those merit tears any time you think of them.

In 1978, Bostonians still maintained an upbeat outlook on life. Locally based television show *Zoom* was still teaching children to use their minds, and Dunkin' Donuts had just opened its 4,000,000[th] area store. But at the same time, fans were still shaken from recent experiences. Twice they had been brought to the precipice of exultation before being yanked back by their replica-jersey collars.

But the current Red Sox team was dynamic and exploded out of the gate, taking a seemingly insurmountable lead over all comers. Literally, *Happy Days* had come to Boston. (The producers of the show were filming a feature on Henry Winkler as he went back to his alma mater, Emerson, to be honored for telling people to sit on it.) Skepticism relinquished its hold on the populace in favor of complacency. And for the rest of the summer, Bostonians spent their time saving their money for playoff tickets.

Meanwhile, 200 miles down I-95 (which at that time had just celebrated its 46th-straight year of road construction), trouble was a-brewin'.

A Threat to the Nation

The New York ballclub was embroiled in turmoil. It was a good ol' fashioned "moil broil." The Yankees' manager, Billy Martin, just wasn't cutting it. After two lackluster years winning just two American League pennants and one World Series, the Yankees' even-tempered owner, George Steinbrenner, had seen enough. The team was 14 games behind the dominant Red Sox and Martin had to go.

FENWAY FACTS

Butch Hobson's real name is Clell Lavern Hobson Jr. He was nicknamed "Butch" by the fans on "Rename a Player Day," held on June 18, 1976.

Steinbrenner decided to install Bob "Big Comeback" Lemon as the new skipper. With a name like that, you'd think Boston would've seen the motion picture rolling in front of them.

Lemon's controversial strategy of winning instead of losing was met with widespread support in New York. The team took to the change immediately and won 19 of their next 27 games. The Red Sox, on the other hand, decided they had too many good players on their team to promote humility and fair sportsmanship, so they traded Bernie Carbo and future Hall of Famer Ferguson Jenkins. And just to be safe, Boston manager Don Zimmer decided against using Bill Lee in the late-season series against the Yankees. Lee's record of 12–5 against the pinstripes was just too solid.

Oh, Really?

"Bucky" is a swear word in Boston. You can be issued a fine if you say it in Brookline.

Ambushed!

That was just the opening the Yankees were looking for. What began as a simple contest on September 7 devolved into one of the most gruesome affairs in the history of Red Sox Nation. To this day, accounts of the events are still conflicting. Many reports claim that early in the game, a Red Sox pitcher started taunting one member of the Yankees about his mother and the type of footwear she wore. Then the pitcher started throwing baseballs toward him to try to get the batsman to give up his ground.

No one can be sure, but at that point someone, probably the third-base coach, flashed the "swing away" sign and all hell broke loose. One batsman swung and got a hit, then another, and another, until there was confusion and pandemonium. Red Sox players were collapsing from the exhaustion of chasing balls around the field.

When it was all over, the Red Sox lay strewn upon a pile of rawhide and tobacco. They didn't know what had hit them. The fans remained stunned as well, barely able to order another round of drinks.

FENWAY FACTS

Legendary public address announcer Sherm Feller always summoned his grandchildren to the dinner table by calling their names, their school grades, and then their names again.

The headline the next morning of the local rag read, "Horrid Massacre in Boston, Perpetrated on the Second Weekend of September, 1978, by the Yankees of the Bronx."

The players came to and found they were now looking up at the surprising New York team from three games behind.

The Final Showdown

Collecting what was left of their dignity, the Red Sox regrouped with the intent of exacting revenge on the marauders from the

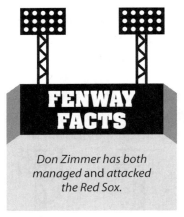

FENWAY FACTS

Don Zimmer has both managed and attacked the Red Sox.

Bronx. And with evil coursing through their veins and a bit of sympathy in their hearts, the Yankees let the Red Sox track them down, setting up a one-game play-off, loser take none. They even allowed the Red Sox to host the game at Fenway Park (and everyone knows how well that went the last time).

The hometown heroes got sucked in again, this time by the Yankees' secret weapon—the winner of their promotional "Play Shortstop for the Yankees" contest. The diminutive Bucky Dent, a librarian by trade, was to Reggie Jackson what Nelson de la Rosa was to Pedro Martinez. But when Boston's pitching star Mike Torrez let down his guard, the shortstop took his club and pounded Torrez's offering over the wall in left field for a three-run homer.

Yankees players start a Hacky Sack circle in front of Carlton Fisk.

It was all the offense New York would need (although they got two more runs courtesy of the guy everyone expected to hit a home run). Boston had been beaten again. And the vil-

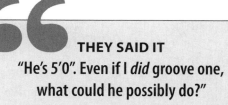

THEY SAID IT

"He's 5'0". Even if I *did* groove one, what could he possibly do?"

—*Mike Torrez on Bucky Dent, October 2, 1978*

lain, who would go down in Nation history alongside the most vile of men, went back to his Dewey Decimal System and now runs a camp for future librarian shortstops down in Florida.

The 86-Year War

Held captive by misery for more than eight decades, forced to listen to the neighboring Empire crow about their good fortune, the Nation was enmeshed in a one-sided cold war. Eventually, weary Nationites rose up and decided they had the power to do as they wanted, and not to play the role of second-class citizens at the mercy of another. No, they deserved the independence granted to almost all other major league teams (sorry, Cubbies).

A small coalition of proud men, fervent in their beliefs, attended the First Continental Conquest, where they set forth to draft articles proclaiming their independence from the Curse of the Bambino that did restrict them. These articles, penned during a beer tasting at Boston Beer Works, became the most famous document in our history—the Declaration of Absolution, thus remitting any penalty that trading Babe Ruth may have had on us.

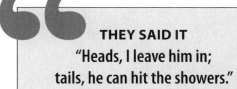

THEY SAID IT

"Heads, I leave him in; tails, he can hit the showers."

—*Grady Little, on whether or not to pull Pedro Martinez from the game early in the eighth inning on October 16, 2003*

The Declaration of Absolution

When in the Course of sporting events it becomes necessary for one group of fans to dissolve the historical binds that have been associated with them and to assume among the powers on the field, the separate but equal ability to consider themselves rivals by the very definition in the Book of Webster and of their entitlement as a franchise in the American League East which does demand a decent respect to no longer be traumatized by the New York Yankees in reference to the Curse of the Bambino.

We hold these truths to be self-evident, that all sports teams are created equal, that they are endowed by their Commissioner.

To prove this, let facts be submitted to a candid world:

- They have chanted "1918."

- They have kicked us, both figuratively and literally, when we were down.

- They have taken great pride in reminding us of 1978.

- They have refused to acknowledge our "rivalry," pointing to its once one-sided nature.

- They have neglected to mention bad calls that allowed them to win.

- They have swooped in and grievously outbid us in requesting the services of free-agent soldiers.

- They have belittled our first five championships because they occurred in "the old days."

- For setting our hats on fire.

- *For cursing at our young and innocent.*

- *For throwing food covered in condiments at us.*

- *For equating our overspending with their egregious overspending.*

- *For no sympathies upon humiliating defeat.*

- *For physical and bodily harm in response to wearing our team colors.*

- *For altogether miscreant behavior unbecoming of adults.*

In every stage of these Oppressions, We have Petitioned for Redress in the most humble terms: our repeated Petitions have been answered only by repeated injury, both bodily and emotionally. A rival, whose character is thus marked by every act may define a Bully, is unfit to be the leader of a Division.

We, therefore, the Representatives of the Nation of Red Sox, in General Assembly over a couple of pitchers of Haymarket Hefe Weizen, appealing to the Supreme Judgment of baseball fans everywhere for the rectitude of our intentions, do, in the Name of the Sox and by Authority of the good people of the Fenway neighborhood, solemnly publish and declare, That this Nation is, and by Right ought to be Free from the Curse and that all taunts from it ought to be totally recanted.

As a free and Independent Nation, we have the Power to win division crowns, purchase high-priced free agents, beat teams in dramatic fashion, and conclude postseason series victoriously, and to do all other Acts and Things which Independent nations may of right do...so there.

Take That!

Shortly after the regime change in 2001, the cold war heated up again as one of our officers fired a shot across the deck of the Empire, smacking its King right in the face as he was placing jelly on his morning scone.

Casualties accumulated by the busload. Fights broke out in the ballpark, heads were pointed to and thrown at (if you can't beat 'em, bean 'em), bullpen employees were harassed, and there was a general uneasiness in the streets.

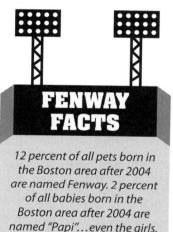

FENWAY FACTS

12 percent of all pets born in the Boston area after 2004 are named Fenway. 2 percent of all babies born in the Boston area after 2004 are named "Papi"...even the girls.

At issue was the validity of the Nation's Declaration. The Empire did not recognize it. Even some loyalists were unsure how change would affect them and were quite happy living under the Curse...until one event changed their minds forever. It took this sudden act, the result of heated emotion and pent-up frustration, to fully win over the hearts and minds of a Nation.

As history has recorded, two officers from the warring armies met to discuss the situation. Officer Alex Rodriguez of the pin-striped blue army defiantly spoke of no such Declaration, at which point Captain Jason Varitek of the red army produced the document, which he kept in his catcher's mitt, and shoved it into Rodriguez's face.

It energized a Nation who, led by First Lieutenant Bill Mueller, began to assert their freedoms over their once-dominant oppressors.

Standing Proudly

When a weary militia rose from the dust and realized that all was calm, it signified a new dawn in the Nation. The representatives of the First Continental Conquest recognized a break from everything they'd held to before and moved forward with newfound confidence.

The 86-Year War was finally ended after one final seven-day battle that culminated with Sergeant Pokey Reese throwing the ball to Private Doug Menkayvitch (pronounced "Mientkiewicz").

The treaty was then signed in St. Louis on October 27, 2004. The signatories had their picture taken for all to see in a pig pile on the mound for *Sports Illustrated* and its annual "Holy Crap, I Can't Believe It Happened" edition. Ever since, Nationites greet each other with a nod and a two-syllable salutation meant to symbolize the hardship they once knew—"Believe." It is a time they will never forget...though, as most were totally wasted, it's a time they have trouble remembering.

Summary

The history of Red Sox Nation offers a lot to absorb. The roller-coaster chronology of this team will always be the most interesting story in town. Tales of redcoats and minutemen battling for land, stockpiles of ammunition, and freedom are old and stale. They've been replaced by epic retellings of pinstripes and sluggers battling for respect and trophies. Each tale boasts nerve-wracking situations, emotional peaks and valleys, and a moral. The moral of this chapter is, with the Red Sox, it's always something.

KEY TERMS

future Yankee [loo'zah] *n*—any good, young player on a small-market team who is looking to make way more money than he could possibly get staying where he is

Red Sox Nation reacts to the reading of the Declaration of Absolution during Historic Comeback Remembrance Day.

Red Sox Nation Time Line

1902—Ban Johnson, founder of the American League, gets Henry Killilea to buy team.

1903—Cy Young comes to camp at age 35 sporting noticeable beer gut; Boston wins World Series.

1906—Americans/Pilgrims/Red Stockings become the Red Sox after eliminating names such as "Indian Slayers," "Drunkards," and "Bojangles."

1908—Cubs win World Series…no, really, they did. We're not kidding.

1912—Boston wins deciding game of the World Series after being down in the tenth inning.

1916—Sox win World Series; Joseph Lannin sells team to Harry Frazee declaring, "Winning bores me."

1919—Sox sell best player, Babe Ruth, to the Yankees.

1933—Tom Yawkey buys the team during the Great Depression; Depression continues for the next 71 years in Boston.

1938—Sox sign amateur fisherman Ted Williams.

1942—In need of a right-field foul pole, Sox sign shortstop Johnny Pesky under the condition that he let them use his.

1946—Sox play extra games in October to "take advantage of Indian summer."

1952—Williams becomes first Triple Crown winner to be shot down while flying an airplane.

1975—Boston celebrates World Series victory after dramatic extra-inning home run before being told they must play one more game, which they lose.

1986—Boston loses potential clinching game of the World Series after being up in the tenth inning.

1992—Jean Yawkey dies; John Harrington denies any wrongdoing, takes over Yawkey Trust anyway.

2001—Yawkey Trust sold to the In-John-Henry-We-Trust Trust.

2002—Williams becomes first Triple Crown winner to have head transported to Arizona via airplane.

2004—Boston fails to acquire Alex Rodriguez; Boston wins the World Series, ending "The Curse of the Bambino."

2006—Outfielder Manny Ramirez battles pulled hamstring, team flounders.

2007—Curt Schilling comes to camp at age 41 sporting a noticeable gut; Boston wins the World Series.

2008—Sox trade best player, Manny Ramirez, to Dodgers; "The Curse of ManRam" begins.

Fun at the Park

Work on this brain teaser:

How could Bob Stanley have a stat line like this and still be considered one of the main scapegoats in Game 6 of the 1986 World Series?

IP	H	R	ER	BB	SO	HR
0	0	0	0	0	0	0

Test Your Knowledge

The Red Sox went 86 years between championships, often losing in the most humiliating fashion, due to:

(A) a curse

(B) bad moves by the front office

(C) umpires conspiring against them

(D) not wanting the Cubs to feel lonely

Did you ever believe the Red Sox would beat the Yankees? No, seriously, did you? You truly believed they would? Honestly? You did? Where were you when it happened? To this day, can you really believe it happened?

Imagine you were one of the delegates at the First Continental Conquest—what would you change or add to the Declaration of Absolution?

3

Architecture

PREREQUISITE

*An ability to pronounce the word **architecture**.*

LEARNING OBJECTIVES

After reading this chapter, you should be able to:

• Explain where the Red Sox's first stadium was

• Imagine how Fenway Park would look today if the original designs were used

• Explain one problem the park had in the 1920s and 1930s

• Understand how the current owners increased revenue

L ocated in the Fenway district of Boston, Fenway Park is truly a national treasure. It's become synonymous with the phrase "the stadium located in the Fenway district of Boston."

It certainly is like no other park in the world. Its "charm and personality" include a fence in center field that juts out from the bullpen, daring fielders to impale themselves upon its corner; seats in foul territory along the right-field line that face right field; poles that sit in front of certain lucky fans; corner infielders that are four bounding steps away from the fans; and, most notably, a giant wall in left field that turns home-run balls into singles.

Was it the designs of a madman or a master craftsman that created what has become a place of worship for millions of Red Sox fans?

1903 B.F. (Before Fenway)

The Red Sox once played at the beautifully groomed Huntington Avenue Grounds on what is now the campus of Northeastern University.

The field was functional. It had a fence. It had stands for 11,500 fans. It even had an overhang to keep some fans from getting drenched by rain or scorched by the sun.

The dimensions were oddly misshapen—the center-field fence was located 530 feet from home plate for the first seven years of its existence, then it was pushed even farther back, to 635 feet. At the same time, they kept the right-field area nice and cozy, placing the fence only 280 feet from the batter. Hence the Boston Americans' first marketing slogan: "Americans Hit it to Right!"

Although the Grounds only hosted games for a short time, it did serve as host for the historic first World Series, welcoming a team from the other side of the world—Pittsburgh.

KEY TERMS

triangle [tri'ang-gl] *n*—the area in center field where balls that would be out of most parks end up bouncing around for in-the-park home runs

A New Owner

After a few years, a new sheriff came to town, and he desired a new ranch. Red Sox owner John Taylor decided to build his own ballpark after the 1910 season. He figured a stadium with a larger capacity would generate more revenue, plus he could get all the hot dogs he wanted on game days.

First he needed a location. Down Huntington Avenue, Brookline Avenue intersected with Boylston Street in a neighborhood known as Fenway. Known for its swampy marshes and marshy swamps, it was perfect for congregating tens of thousands of people together while charging them for parking.

FENWAY FACTS

Fenway Park tours last one hour and include a try-out for shortstop.

With its close proximity to several colleges (Red Sox University began in the back of a butchery two blocks east of Kenmore Square), several of those new-fangled trolley stops, and an array of watering holes, Taylor had found his ideal location.

Now all he needed to do was squeeze an entire major league baseball park between five asymmetrical city streets.

Original Plans

Fenway has always been known for its intimate dimensions, where fans are closer to the players than some of the umpires are.

When deciding on a designer for his new park, Taylor called the finest architects of his time together to discuss his vision. No one returned his calls.

Taylor wanted to copy the blueprints local architect Charles Bulfinch used for the state capitol located on Beacon Hill, but he wasn't allowed to put a gold dome on top of the park. That's reserved for capitol buildings representing the states from where presidents have hailed, he was informed.

Much consideration was put into every feature of the new park. For example, Taylor was not a fan of President William Howard Taft and didn't want a man that large sitting comfortably in his seat. Hence, Taylor opted for the snug-sized seats he located at the Seat Emporium (currently the Borders located near the Public Gardens on Boylston).

As for the famous wall in left, Taylor wrote in his diary that he awoke one night after dreaming of a huge fence in left field and a tiny one in right that symbolized the class differences between the working class and the wealthy. General Charles H. Taylor, John's father, loved the idea of the wall; ever since the Civil War ended, the former commander was still fearful that the South would rise again. He believed the wall would protect the left fielder from invading Confederates. To set his father's paranoid mind at ease, John considered putting spikes on the wall that might protect his players from an advancing army.

In the end, he settled for advertising.

A Spiritual Place

Fenway Park has come to be known as "the Chapel." This is ironic because one of Taylor's ideas was to install tinted glass throughout the park. The colorful material played an important role in architecture in the early 1900s. Of course, much of the world's most beautiful stained glass windows reside in places where baseballs are not hurtling through them. The price of repair would have cost as much as the park itself.

One last attempt to add a regal, timeless feel to his ballpark found Taylor planning to build an arcade—a series of arches supported by columns—from the dugout to home plate. Unfortunately, there were several flaws with that idea, not the least of which was thinking Greek architecture was timeless.

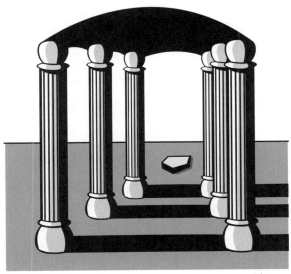

Vito

Citgo sign [see'it'go sine] *n*—a giant sign that says "Citgo"

The Final Design

Pie-in-the-sky dreams gave way to cost-effectiveness and durability. The structure, with Taylor's blessing, was designed by Osborn Engineering and built by James McLaughlin Construction for the bargain price of just $650,000.

When drawing the outfield fences, the Osborn Engineering group had a sudden shortage of protractors and settled for drafting the outfield fence by hand. Unfortunately, their lead architect on the project was sick that day and the chore fell to Charlton "Crazy Eyes" Muskell. With Muskell sketching the dimensions, Fenway's fences ended up distanced thusly from home plate:

Left field: 310 feet
Left center: 379 feet
Center field: 390 feet
Deep center: 420 feet
Right center: 383 feet
Right field: 380 feet
Right-field line: 302 feet

Green Monster [mon'stah] *n*—a 30-foot high inanimate object with mystical powers that turns home runs into doubles and doubles into singles; formerly a break room for Manny Ramirez

April 20, 1912

Due to inclement weather, Fenway opened without much fanfare two days after it was supposed to. The park quickly became embroiled in a huge controversy, gaining itself a degree of infamy it did not deserve.

Five days before Fenway Park opened, the *Titanic* sunk, leaving many actors, including Leonardo DiCaprio, dead. Thankfully, Kate Winslet survived and kept his memory alive. By the time she and the other survivors arrived in New York City, the news agencies had jumped all over the story. The outrage over losing such a marquee movie star was too much to take and many people linked the ship's tragic demise to the park's grand opening.

The public relations team at Fenway worked overtime until they finally managed to pin the blame on Detroit's Navin Field, which

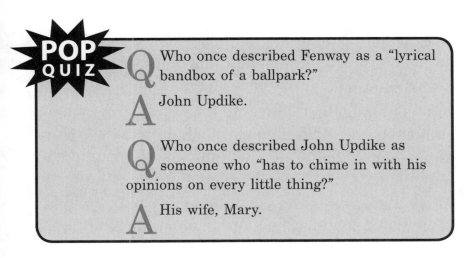

POP QUIZ

Q Who once described Fenway as a "lyrical bandbox of a ballpark?"

A John Updike.

Q Who once described John Updike as someone who "has to chime in with his opinions on every little thing?"

A His wife, Mary.

Oh, Really?

Fenway added lights in 1947. It was a whopping 45 years before Camden Yards, a supposedly modern stadium, did. That's progressive!

had opened on the same day. In their own attempt to disassociate themselves with the sinking of the largest passenger ship and one of the most expensive movies ever made, the Tigers changed their park's name to Briggs Stadium and then Tigers Stadium, finally having to close it down due to the public outcry a mere 88 years after it opened.

But as Celine Dion says, Fenway will go on.

THE GREEN MONSTER

Some interesting facts about baseball's most famous wall:

- It wasn't always green. It used to be covered by ads. (Hard to look at the wall these days and imagine it covered by old-fashioned ads. You'd have to use your imagination to strip away the current ads.)

- It now stands at 37′2″ tall, exactly one inch shorter than a Bucky Dent homer.

- It used to be only 25 feet high, growing out of the high point of a 10-foot slope in left field nicknamed "Duffy's Cliff" for the left fielder who mastered the nuances of playing it, Cliff Lewis.

- Manny Ramirez used to take breaks inside the wall. He had a vending machine and coffee maker installed there to take full advantage of his players union–mandated five-minute break for every fly ball caught.

Renovations Through the Years

From the outset, the combination of the fence's flammability and a patronage that loved to bring their binoculars to the game caused problems. In 1926, fans holding their binoculars up to the sun directed the magnified glare toward the unsuspecting seats and set them ablaze. The wooden bleachers in left field were quickly vacuumed up and removed, increasing the size of the foul territory.

A young upstart named Tom Yawkey took over the team in 1933. Unfortunately, those who do not learn the lessons of history are doomed to repeat them. Thinking the "Warning: Extremely Flammable" signs on the wall were simply public service announcements, Yawkey ignored the notice.

The second fire in a decade came on January 5, 1934, and this one was far bigger. It destroyed much of the park and the wall that gave Fenway its identity.

Yawkey worked quickly to rebuild it, this time leaving no safety measure to chance. At first, he tried a wall of straw, and then a wall of sticks, but wolves were constantly on the prowl along Lansdowne Street trying to blow the wall down. He eventually found that a wall of wood covered in tin and concrete would be his solution. And he made the grandstands out of concrete and steel.

Two years later, after parking his car on the roof of a parking garage across Lansdowne Street, Yawkey's windshield was smashed by a towering batting-practice home run. He decided to add a screen over the Monster.

KEY TERMS

the Fisk Stick [fisk stick**]** *n*—the bright yellow pole at the end of the left-field foul line (it isn't actually called "the Fisk Stick," but we think it should be)

A ROOM WITH NO VIEW

The renovations at Fenway left unresolved the issue of **obstructed-view seats.** Yawkey had been stuck with them since he bought the club. He thought about removing the poles, but was told that would cause the roof to collapse. He wanted to drill peepholes in them before deciding against it. He even bandied around the idea of having crow's nests attached 20 feet above the obstructed-view seats, but he thought that would be better suited to the Pirates' stadium.

Yawkey would keep his wife up at night searching for an answer to the problem, eventually wearing the rug down so much he turned his attention from fixing the poles to figuring out how to fix his rug. And to this day, the obstructed-view seats remain.

It wasn't until 1940 that an owner figured out how to cater Fenway's dimensions to his star players. Yawkey added the bullpens in right field in order to give Ted Williams a short fence to aim for and to prevent any opposing fielder patrolling the ground in center from living out his projected lifespan.

If You Build More, They Will Come

For the better part of seven decades, the Yawkeys and their Trust ran the Red Sox, and the thought of moving the team out of Fenway didn't enter anyone's consciousness. But then the team was sold to John Henry and his band of merry men. A possible move was back on the table.

The new owners looked at many different options, ranging from a new park in the same spot to a new park on the Waterfront, where future Dodgers owner and real estate developer Frank McCourt held the cards. Since they spent a record gajillion dollars (approximately) to buy the team, they had to figure a way to earn back as much revenue as possible. Charging $400 for a hot dog was an option, but they reasoned it might be better to increase the capacity of the park.

With the help of Janet Marie Smith, the architect who worked on Camden Yards, there was no shortage of ideas about where to add more seats.

They considered a row of seats behind the second-base bag.

They experimented
with hot-air balloon
seats, but didn't want
to upset the FAA.

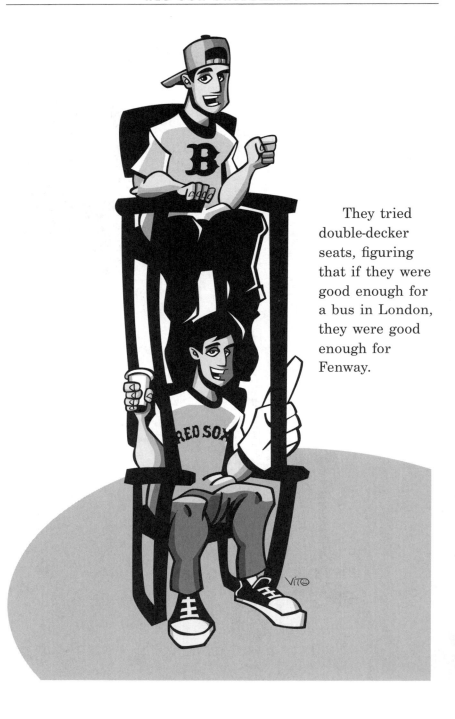

They tried double-decker seats, figuring that if they were good enough for a bus in London, they were good enough for Fenway.

They even considered a row of seats in the dugout next to the players, but with beer sales cut off after the seventh inning, that would've gotten real ugly, real fast.

Stumped, they brainstormed one evening until late in the night, sustained only by Dunkin' Donuts coffee Coolattas and little slider burgers from Game On! Finally, someone asked the assistant taking notes, "What do you think, Annette?"

At that point, Larry Lucchino jumped up and said, "That's it!" knocking over the boxes of Munchkins still waiting to be opened. "Not a net, but *the* net. We'll get rid of the net!" And that's when the idea of the Monster seats was born. And with the 274 seats within spitting distance of any left fielder roaming the grounds, a new era was born for the Grand Ole Ballpark.

KEY TERMS

bleacher creature [bleech'ah creech'ah]
n—one who sits in the bleachers

A fan in the Monster seats celebrates after correctly guessing the game's attendance.

Home Sweet Home

As it is now, the park's capacity has been increased about 8 percent. This added some much-needed capital to the team's coffers. One thing that didn't pan out was putting names on the players' home jerseys, then selling the naming rights on all their players. This failed after Trot Giant Glass's agent filed an injunction against the team.

The notion that Fenway Park embodies the heart of its denizens reminds one of the age-old question: which came first, the chicken or the omelet? Was the park molded to fit the personality of the fans, or did the fans come to mold themselves to the unbending image of the park?

Q According to Dennis "Oil Can" Boyd, which American League ballpark was built on the ocean?

A Cleveland's Municipal Stadium, located on the banks of the Lake Erie Ocean.

Great architects have said that they build their structures to reflect the values and ideals of the people who live, work, or visit there. Look at the other parks in the league and you'll see the truth in that statement.

The Metrodome in Minneapolis is white and temperature-controlled, just like Minnesotans.

Oakland's McAfee Coliseum, the home for the Athletics, is more of a football stadium than a ballpark. The expansive foul territory makes it feel as if the fans aren't even there, which suits them because they aren't.

As for Yankee Stadium...nah, too easy.

Summary

Fenway embodies the culture that surrounds it and the nature of the fans who walk through the turnstiles every night. It might not be perfect, but there's something about the oak chairs that are a chiropractor's meal ticket, the narrow rows that require a ballet fellowship in order to navigate, or the idea of only being

KEY TERMS

bleachers [bleech'ahs] *n*—the seats located in center field; where the wave begins

able to see certain aspects of a game (like a line drive down the line in left).

Say What?

"Manny being Manny"—common euphemism for "What can you do?" It was originally used to describe Manny Ramirez and his penchant for doing weird things, but it has now become part of baseball culture.

After being given life by John Taylor, the little park in the soggy, buggy, marsh-ridden neighborhood adjacent to the Emerald Necklace has given life to its fans and has held them for almost half a century, through the heart-stomping bad times and the equally heart-stomping great times. DiCaprio couldn't have done that.

KEY TERMS

red seat [seat of red] *n*—the seat struck by the longest home run ever at Fenway, hit by Ted Williams; a seat in right field that is routinely passed over by balls hit by David Ortiz

RED SOX

Fun at the Park

As a student here at the University, you should plan to visit the hallowed field as much as possible in order to familiarize yourself with each special nook and cranny.

Test Your Knowledge

If the Red Sox decide to add more seats to Fenway Park, where could they put them?

Taking into consideration the deep corner in right (and its potential for ricochets), the vast triangle in center, and the wall in left, which outfield position seems like it would be the hardest to play?

Kenmore or Harvard Avenue in Brighton—which is the better place to light things on fire during a victory celebration?

Would you rather watch a series-clinching game from an obstructed-view seat or on a big-screen TV at home?

4

Government

Government: A Range of Subjects

Government is probably the most intensive and thorough curriculum here at the University, and this chapter covers the whole field better than Jacoby Ellsbury. As a citizen of the Nation, you may think to yourself, *How can we, mere plebeians, have our voices heard? How did we get here? Why can't I call another team's general manager and propose a trade for my team?*

All valid questions, save for the last one, and since *SportsCenter* starts soon (whenever you're reading this, it's a pretty safe bet that *SportsCenter* starts soon), we're going to bypass the cocktail weenies and get right to the lobster roll.

Our National Government

Red Sox Nation has a well-developed government that rules its actions. Over the years, there have been vast changes in structure and regulations. There was a time when the harshest law our citizens faced was **"No Pepper."** Now you can't have pepper, salt, cinnamon, mint, basil, parsley, sage, rosemary, or thyme. How did it get to this point?

The populace of the Nation is comprised of very different factions, and it is the goal of the government to keep those factions united, in times of win streaks and losing streaks equally.

The government was put in place to (1) field a team, and (2) keep the team away from the citizens who want to run it. Of course, if the citizens ran it, they might spend all their money on high-priced free agents, but that money is better spent on **Jimmy Fund** donations and playoff apparel. So the government puts people in cushy offices to keep the citizens from making fools of themselves. The government tries to make them happy by adding

KEY TERMS

No Pepper [no peppah] *n*—the words formerly written on the wall directly behind home plate, they were replaced by capitalist propaganda, thus allowing the team to sign high-priced free agents

RED SOX NATION FACTS IN BRIEF

- **Capital:** The Fens, Massachusetts
- **Global Population:** Lots; fluctuates based on how the team is doing
- **Currency:** The castiglione (1 US Dollar = 117 castigliones)
- **Form of Government:** Constitutional Monarchy
- **Executive:** Majority owner, other owners, chief executive officer, RSN president (figurehead)
- **Judiciary:** Commissioner of baseball, kangaroo court for clubhouse issues
- **Legislative:** Composed of hundreds of scribes, beat reporters, columnists, bloggers, talk-radio hosts, talk-radio callers, whiner-line participants, etc.
- **Major Religion:** Soxism
- **Climate:** Cool, then hot, then windy, muggy, wet, then hot again, a little icy, more heat, followed by wind and a cool heat
- **Equator:** Lies directly in the middle of the bleachers, where temperatures have been known to reach 150 degrees
- **Precipitation:** The only precipitation is from the Beer Man, or the sweaty guy seated behind you
- **Primary export:** Opinions, enthusiasm

or subtracting players (but never dividing or multiplying them), thus shielding its citizens from blame should such moves falter.

When John Henry and his friends purchased the team for $700 million, one of their first acts was to enact a Constitution. The drafters made sure to include 10 amendments—a Bill of Rights—allowing its citizens rights they had never been entitled to before.

KEY TERMS

Jimmy Fund [jim'mee fund] *n*—the charity set up for Jimmy and all his friends; a great cause

The Bill of Rights

Amendment I

Ownership shall make no law respecting an establishment of religion, or prohibiting the free exercise thereof. (Though it is highly recommended that you follow Soxism lest your season tickets be moved behind a pole.)

Or abridging the freedom of speech in the form of a "Yankees Suck" chant or calling WEEI to complain about the manager's latest move, his lack of a move, his desire to move, his patience to move, his moving to move, his putting his house on the market to move, etc. The press is allotted these same freedoms. (Yes, even Dan Shaughnessy.)

Or the right of the people to assemble peaceably. The key and operative word here, people, is *peaceably*. Once that dumb guy from Allston starts climbing the lamppost and throwing bottles at riot police, all bets are off.

And to petition the government for a redress of grievances as long as the petition comes in the form of a banner, poster, or five friends painting their bodies so their message is seen when they take their shirts off.

Amendment II

The right of the people to keep beers in their arms shall not be infringed until two and a half hours after first pitch.

Amendment III

No fan shall in time of season be refused tickets short of available resources.

Amendment IV

No search and seizures of memorabilia by any fan, Red Sox or otherwise. There shall be no defacing, scuffing, marking, devaluing, or swiping of any Red Sox–related items.

Amendment V

No person shall be held to answer for a capital, or otherwise infamous crime such as changing seats during a rally, changing underwear during a winning streak, or not burning your clothes during a losing streak; nor shall any person be subject for blame for any event occurring on the field ("the Bartman Clause").

Amendment VI

In all media avenues, the devoted shall have frequent access to up-to-the-minute scores pertaining in all fashions to the Red Sox, and also the Yankees.

Amendment VII

In arbitration of common argument, the right of each party to be either positive or negative is allowed. Disagreement is welcomed to keep a steady balance.

Amendment VIII

Excessive viewing of torturous moments from Game 6, nor excessive reminiscing be imposed unless a desired outcome was achieved, nor cruel and unusual punishment.

Amendment IX

The enumeration in the Constitution, of certain rights, shall not be construed to deny or disparage others retained by the people...provided there are no ties to Yankees fans.

Amendment X

The powers not delegated to the Nation by the Constitution nor prohibited by it are reserved to the people individually.

Executive Branch

The head of Red Sox Nation is the team's ownership group, led by John Henry (no relation to John Henry, the steel-drivin' man), chairman Tom Werner (no relation to Werner Klemperer, who played Col. Klink on *Hogan's Heroes*), and CEO Larry Lucchino (who is related to everybody). There are also many partners in this endeavor; in fact, check your mail—you might be one, too.

These men controlled all the decision-making power until the first democratic election in this Nation's history was held. There were speeches, bloggings, campaigning, and even a debate; at the end stood one man—the president of the Nation, Jerry Remy.

It is the job of President Remy to broadcast games, do commercials, wear a mustache, pose for bobbleheads, make Don Orsillo laugh, mispronounce difficult names like "Saltalamacchia," and greet fans who fawn over him so much that they get spittle on his tie. He's also allowed to talk policy with the owners.

As we will learn in economics, it is the front office that deals with the budget and salary cap concerns. Budgets are strictly adhered to using almost military-like discipline; the agreed-upon budget will not be breached under any circumstances...unless a player that the club really wants becomes available. In that case, the budget will be raised and then will not be breached under any circumstance.

KEY TERMS

Remdawg [rem'ee] *n*—an amiable non-canine whose bark is worse than his broadcast

Red Sox front-office members take turns watching Larry Lucchino hold the World Series trophy.

Legislative Branch

These are the representatives who help us voice our opinions. They have little to no power, but at least we can speak to them. It's much more feasible than trying to go through the president.

This branch of government is open 24 hours a day through e-mail, telephone, online chats, or throughout town if you happen to run into them. They have access to the executive branch through their press credentials and can pass along your thoughts. On occasion, they will even introduce a bill to them, such as "The Win Now Act," which proposes trading away prospects for a right-handed, power-hitting outfielder to help get the Red Sox to the World Series. But there's never any guarantee that the executive branch will ever consider the proposal, and the bill will most likely die on the floor of the sports bar Game On!

But these representatives are our mouthpieces. They carry with them the various opinions of you, the Nationites, and have a pulpit on which to relay those opinions—the AM radio dial and late-night sports shows. Each stakes claim to a viewpoint and recites it passionately. They talk and talk and talk and talk, and when they're done talking, they pass the microphone off to another senator to talk for them. The beauty of their forum is that none of them can be held accountable for what they've said or predictions that they've made. They simply utter the phrase, "That is not what I said," and all will be forgiven, regardless of

Ask the Valedictorian

Do you have any advice for calling into a talk-radio program?

Talk radio has two major components: talking and radio, though you'd do yourself a favor to ignore the second half of that. Here are some helpful hints:

- Turn your radio down. Similarly, move away from any children, infants, animals, or emergency vehicles.

- Don't say anything stupid. You can disagree with the hosts, but if you suggest that Big Papi was only a good hitter when Manny was hitting behind him, your credibility meter goes down the drain.

- Don't drive through bad cell zones while you're on the phone.

- Do not try to be funny.

- Don't waste time telling the hosts how great you think they are.

- Don't go off on a one-sided rant. That's for callers on Jim Rome's show, and they're listening to Jim Rome so you don't have to.

- Bring something to the table. Don't just agree or disagree with someone.

- Work quickly, be engaging, have fun, and don't be a moron. Even if you're depressed that the Red Sox have lost one in a row, smile.

any audio or video tape of them saying it. Recorded material is not admissible in a court of law.

Ye Public

Finally, there are the masses. The masses tend to fall politically on one of two sides—liberal or conservative. Where do you fall along the political spectrum?

Liberals	Conservatives
fraternize with Yankees fans on non-game days; talk about a possible win before the final out; pro-"wave"; in favor of re-signing free agents; respect Jeter; endorse a salary cap.	advocate fewer rules, including no beer cut-off; pro-"Yankees Suck" chant; favor big payroll; boo their own players; hold grudges; anti-revenue sharing.

Internal Relations

On occasion, the Red Sox clubhouse experiences insubordination, a coup, a mutiny, or other internal squabbles. These distractions can come in many forms, including player-on-player violence, player-on-manager violence, and player-on–clubhouse furniture violence. When this happens, it is the job of the government,

POP QUIZ

Q Which of the four players shipped to Florida for Mike Lowell and Josh Beckett did not have an accent in his name?

A Hanley Ramirez, who went on to become the National League's Rookie of the Year in 2006. Ramirez was traded with Jesús Delgado, Harvey García, and Anibal Sánchez.

from the highest levels down to the lowest, to cover up any hint of unrest.

To the media, dissension is like saccharin to an insect. That's why the press is only allowed into the players' quarters during "happy play time," when all the players pretend everything is wonderful and everyone is getting along well.

There are times, however, when emotional explosions can't be hidden—anytime Carl Everett enters a room, for example. More recently, Manny Ramirez was seen on television taking a swing at Kevin Youkilis in the Red Sox dugout. This got taken totally out of context, as it was later learned Manny caught Youk's goatee out of the corner of his eye and mistook it for a deadly tarantula. Nevertheless, the public called for strict action as a poll taken the day after demonstrated:

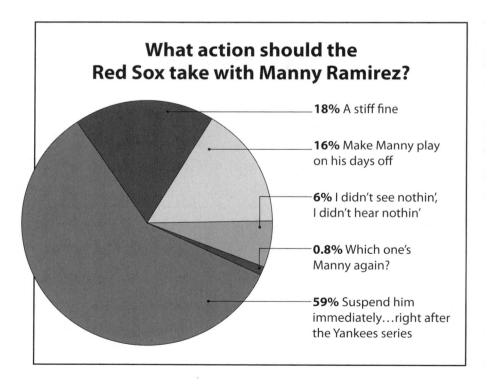

What action should the Red Sox take with Manny Ramirez?

18% A stiff fine

16% Make Manny play on his days off

6% I didn't see nothin', I didn't hear nothin'

0.8% Which one's Manny again?

59% Suspend him immediately...right after the Yankees series

Internal relations are important because the Nation is built upon the public's perception of the team remaining positive. In the end, it's best to let the harsh hand of the law handle these situations, as the information disseminated might not be complete. (Ask George W. Bush about taking action based on unsubstantiated evidence.)

Political Theory and Philosophy

General managers are the baseball equivalents of the head of the Joint Chiefs of Staff. The Red Sox have employed some good ones; none ever seem perfect, and they each come in with their own philosophies.

Dick O'Connell built up the farm system beginning in the 1960s and created a team that was competitive throughout the 1970s and included MVPs, a Rookie of the Year, and some dominant starting pitching.

Dan Duquette, on the other hand, liked to shop at Building 19 for his roster. He ignored the farm system and spent his time looking for bargains on the discount rack. He found some lightly regarded players that turned out okay, including Tim Wakefield and Troy O'Leary. He used the farm system to make trades like the one that brought Pedro Martinez over from Montreal.

Theo Epstein and his staff are very pro-development. They see great advantage to cultivating the farm system. It helps to have tens of millions of dollars to sign free agents, but that's not their primary focus.

THEY SAID IT

"Three queens beats your two pair. You've got to give us Derek Lowe and Jason Varitek for Heathcliff Slocumb now."

—Boston GM Dan Duquette to Seattle GM Woody Woodward on July 31, 1997

Oh, Really?

Lou Gorman is the only man to build a World Series team that defeated his own World Series team (1986).

It's all a matter of one's philosophy and outlook on the game. In the game of Stratego, do you put your flag on the back flank and surround it with bombs, or do you place it in a less obvious spot and position a general next to it? These are all questions that the head of the Joint Chiefs must consider.

Comparative Governments

The government of Red Sox Nation might be the gold standard across the league, but it's certainly not the only model for governance. Each franchise oversees its fans with different rules and hierarchies. For example, the Yankees employ a straight monarchy (not a dictatorship, though some of those rules apply as well) where King George, now retired, and his princes Hal and Hank reign over disgruntled subjects who live in fear of their leaders blowing a gasket every time the Yankees lose a game.

Each government must take into consideration its citizens' needs, interests, and concerns. All teams look at the world differently and therefore a government that might not seem viable to us could be the most efficient ruling body available for that particular region.

Political Behavior

Political behavior in the Nation is often influenced by the actions of other teams. Past governments believed in transaction without reaction; that is, just because another team bettered themselves doesn't mean the Red Sox should keep pace.

It's been said that the best transaction is the one not made, but a government must determine the merits of that position in

Priorities of Sports Fans in Various Cities

BOSTON	LOS ANGELES	WASHINGTON, D.C.	NASHVILLE
• The Red Sox	• Movies	• Politics	• Local news
• Politics of the Red Sox	• Movies about sports	• Politicians at sporting events	• Politics
• Red Sox fans overseas	• Making a sports event into a movie	• How to politicize a sporting event to your advantage	• Finance
• Weather at the Sox game	• Angelina Jolie's new baby	• How to turn a sporting event into a fundraiser	• Weather
• The Patriots and Celtics	• Maximizing profit of sports movies	• What's Bill Clinton up to now?	• Sports

each individual case. Any dynamic shift in the balance of power could be seen by the public as disastrous, so usually something has to be done. That's how Manny Ramirez ended up with the Red Sox after Mike Mussina had signed with the Yankees, and why, upon losing out on Carl Pavano (also to the Yankees), the Red Sox went after and signed Matt Clement.

As you can see, sometimes reaction is good, and sometimes... not so much.

Summary

The Nation's current government has been forged after many hardships. The blueprint of every past administration has been studied, and the current leadership is trying not to make the same mistakes their forebears made. The citizens of Red Sox Nation are currently enjoying a culture of prosperity virtually unheard of in our history.

The diagram of our government holds many lessons, but the key is for each generation to learn the lessons of the past. Hence, you've been granted a lot of power by the government, and all they ask in return is for you to stop calling Billy Beane in Oakland and pretending to be Theo Epstein.

Fun at the Park

Name some former Red Sox players who had a more acclaimed brother on another team. (For example, we had Mike Maddux, while brother Greg played elsewhere.)

Test Your Knowledge

How would you run the team differently?

If you could add an 11th Amendment to our Bill of Rights, what would it be?

Can the concept of transaction without reaction be applied to things other than the Red Sox? If so, what are some examples?

5

Statistics & Probability

PREREQUISITE

Counting to the number 10.

LEARNING OBJECTIVES

After reading this chapter, you should be able to:

• Understand how the front office and fans use stats differently

• List important statistics from the past, as well as more modern measures

• Calculate any equation pertaining to baseball players and their effectiveness

• Join a rotisserie league and win

A recent study of 890 Red Sox fans found that just over 146 percent of them didn't like math and found routine concepts such as percentages tough to grasp.

Unfortunately for them, it's part of the core curriculum here at the University. In fact, statistics and probability contain among the most important lessons to be gleaned from this higher body of gleaning. One must master the fundamentals if one's ultimate goal is to pursue a career running the Red Sox.

We'll try to make it as painless as possible.

Why Stats are Prevalent

Numbers are more a part of this game than any other. Baseball is perfect for statisticians who live to keep a number of records and records of numbers, manipulating each and every combination, permutation, interpretation, and all the other –ations that transpire during the course of the game. It might be due to the fact that there's an inordinate amount of time during a baseball game when, frankly, nothing's happening. Author Edward Abbey observed that, "Baseball is a slow game with frequent and trivial interruptions, offering the spectator many opportunities to reflect at leisure upon the situation on the field." Hence, you can record stats, talk about stats, reminisce about stats, compare stats, and even create new stats.

When we speak of keeping stats, we're not talking about scoring the game here. By scoring the game, we mean writing down everything that happens in shorthand descriptions that only those scoring the game can interpret. (We'll briefly cover that later in this chapter.) RSU does offer advanced courses in game scoring, but that's for neither the faint of heart nor the restless of energy.

Putting Numbers to Good Use

Knowing what stats are kept is only half the battle. What's crucial is to use them to understand what teams are thinking, both on the field and in the front office. In a later chapter, we will delve further into how the mighty dollar impacts player transactions, but most conversations begin with the percentage points and round numbers of *los statísitcos!*

To Each Their Own

To management, stats help determine a player's value; once a player is acquired, the front-office dwellers defer to the manager to best utilize the player's talents. Baseball's unwritten rules do not allow the front office to make in-game decisions (Steinbrenners excepted, of course).

Fans, too, use stats, but usually in an effort to second-guess management, make predictions to impress their friends, or entertain themselves by spouting unimportant numbers for hours and hours. Warning: the study of stats might also contribute to the loss of one's significant other.

A Matter of Historic Importance

Members of the media also use numbers to measure the legacy of a player. Voting members into the Hall of Fame is subjective—baseball writers are under no obligation to vote one way or the other—but voters should exercise the utmost impartiality in making a responsible decision. And that requires a player's lifetime tallies.

Look at the case of Roger Clemens and his pending addition to the Hall of Fame ballot. There are many stats to study and lots of questions to be asked: How many wins did he get? Was his ERA comparable to other members

> **THEY SAID IT**
> "Barring the use of performance-enhancing drugs, Roger Clemens is, without a doubt, in the 'twilight of his career.'"
> —Boston GM Dan Duquette in 1996

already enshrined in Cooperstown? Was that girl of age? Were they just friends? Was that bat he threw at Mike Piazza during a game just friendly gamesmanship or a display of roid rage? In the end, Clemens' entry into the Hall of Fame will come down to one statistic: the number of Southern Republicans there are on the voting committee.

The Basics

Let's start easy: in the olden days, batters were measured by three main statistics—batting average (BA), home runs (HR), and runs batted in (RBI). Batting average is determined by dividing the number of a player's hits by the number of his at-bats. Reaching base due to an error or walk or being hit by a pitch do not count as at-bats, even though they occurred while the player was at bat. (Sorry, we said we'd start easy. These rules are a bit confusing.)

Oh, Really?

Former Red Sox third baseman and Hall of Famer Wade Boggs became the first major leaguer to get pantsed by the gang at Cheers. He is also the only person to hit a homer for his 3,000th hit.

Other popular stats included hits, walks, strikeouts, and the number of times a player grounded into a double play (GIDP), but those were less relevant to the baseball minds of that time. Remember, this was before free agency put pressure on the front office to make high-priced decisions, which would eventually put an increased focus on the value of stats.

The Triple Crown of Hitting

Leading the league in batting average, home runs, and RBI is known as winning the Triple Crown. This achievement has only been accomplished 15 times in baseball history, none more impressive than the first-ever man to do it, Paul Hines of the Providence

WHY ARE RELIEVERS CALLED "FIREMEN"?

Relievers are typically called in to figuratively "put out the fire." That is, their job is to come in when a little spark, such as a bloop single or a double into the gap, might ignite a conflagration or rally. They extinguish the spark...or at least give a talk to their team about fire prevention. Well, that and because of the time former Red Sox closer Mike Fornieles *literally* put out the fire. Seems weak-hitting catcher and future weak-hitting team owner Haywood Sullivan was the victim of a hot foot gone awry in the bullpen one afternoon in 1960.

Today, closers usually come in for the save in the ninth inning and sometimes in the eighth. Yankees legend and frequent Red Sox rag doll Mariano Rivera is known for entering in the eighth inning. He's the exception and he's tempting fate. If he's not careful, he's going to blow his arm out by the time he's 75. That'll learn him.

Finally, after much complaining to the Fireman's Union (F.U.), relievers who pitched well but did not receive credit for a save were given something called a "hold." Holds measure the number of times a pitcher enters with a lead and doesn't give it up, or, better put, leaves after just doing his job.

Grays in 1878. Hines smacked a whopping four homers, knocked in 50 runs, and batted .358 to set the bar outrageously high for any batter with absolutely no power to conquer.

Though rare now, Triple Crown winners used to be much more common; there was a long stretch between 1966 and 1967 when a Triple Crown was won each year. Two members of the Red Sox have won the right to call themselves Triple Crowners: Ted Williams (1942, 1947) and Carl Yastrzemski (1967).

The Triple Crown of Pitching

Pitchers were also largely measured by only three statistics—Earned Run Average, strikeouts, and wins. ERA is like golf: the lower the number, the better. The name is misleading, though. As a pitcher, you really don't *earn* any runs. You give up runs or are blamed for the runs. It should really be termed Blamed Run Average. But describing a pitcher's BRA would make it way too easy for the beat reporters to lose focus on writing serious pieces.

A Glut of Stats

In recent years, baseball stat sheets read more like a company's prospectus and now have more numbers than a drum full of Lotto balls.

You can make a ratio for any two stats, really. BB/K is the number of walks received for every strikeout. 1B/GS is the number of singles for every grand slam slammed. BS/HT is, of course, the number of bats splintered to every holdout threatened by a player. GO/TL measures ground outs per every torn ligament a player has suffered. And TR/IF is the number of tickets requested by a player per the number of members in his immediate family. (That's an important stat for the traveling secretary.)

And then, without warning, came the integration between simple, wholesome baseball stats and complex, evil calculus.

Moneyball

Recently, a new breed of stat geeks stormed onto the scene wearing pocket protectors and taped-together glasses. They turned the baseball world on its ear and ushered in a new era of player scouting.

 **KEY TERMS**

small ball [smallball] *n*—a baseball strategy that involves boring the crowd by not hitting home runs

Ask the Valedictorian

How many games can the Red Sox lose during a seven-game series before you should start to worry?

Well, the Red Sox *are* the only team in the history of baseball to come back from a 3–0 deficit to win a series. They not only lost the first three games, but they lost the third game by 11 runs. They triumphed after hitting the part of the earth just *below* rock bottom. So anything is possible. That said, while you shouldn't start worrying after every loss, you should start complaining about it immediately.

Everything changed when Bill James came to town. "Wild Bill," they called him, the father of modern baseball statistics. The Kansas native and baseball writer has turned player evaluation on its ear with formulas that allow anyone to determine what will happen for sure, without a doubt...unless it doesn't happen that way.

Sabermetrics started to become the predominant way to measure a player's performance or potential. The field was named after former Red Sox pitcher Bret Saberhagen, whose name comes from the Dutch word *SABR*, meaning Society for American Baseball Research, and *hagendaas*, meaning ice cream.

KEY TERMS

seeing-eye single [see'ying I sing'gull] *n—* a batted ball that narrowly evades the reach of more than one infielder on its way to the outfield for a base hit; a single that assists blind people

Billy Beane, momentary general manager of the Red Sox whose first and only transaction was to resign as general manager of the Red Sox in 2003, was deified in Michael Lewis' book, *Moneyball*, bringing the new stats to light and thus rendering the old way of looking at stats obsolete.

The Golden Stat

One stat has emerged from the pack to become the "chosen one"—on-base percentage (OBP). This is the percentage of time that a player reaches base. On-base percentage does not take into consideration his time in the bathroom, at home, playing with his kids at the beach, sleeping in the clubhouse, or other non-ballgame activities. Otherwise, the percentages would be far lower, since a player only spends a few minutes of his waking hours on base. For example, assuming he gets a healthy eight hours of sleep per night, Dustin Pedroia would have an on-base percentage of just .0052.

The Red Sox *love* this stat. If the governor legalized inter-pronounal marriages and allowed humans to marry stats, most members of the Red Sox front office would pick this stat to be their lawfully wedded significant other.

Batting average is so passé, what with its average of batting and all. OBP is the new darling. It includes walks. It's the difference between a chocolate sundae with whipped cream and a chocolate sundae with whipped cream *and* nuts. (Unless you're allergic to nuts, in which case you should stay away from on-base percentage.)

OBP comprises half of another popular new stat: OPS, or *on-base plus slugging*. To determine a player's OPS, one must know what his slugging percentage (or SLG) is. That's the total bases per at-bat. (Note that is not meant to imply the number of bases *on the field* per every at-bat.)

For example, here are Manny Ramirez's percentages in 2008 (Boston/L.A.):

Batting average—.332

Slugging percentage—.601

OBP—.430

OPS—1.031

What does it all mean? No one knows for sure, but while studies are being conducted, these numbers support agent Scott Boras' argument in contract negotiations: "My client should earn $20 million a year because his OPS has numbers on *both* sides of the decimal point." And no one has been able to counter that argument yet, so he usually gets what he wants.

Stats for the Fans

Stats are generally regarded differently by the fans than they are by the front office. The fans pay for the fireworks display. Chicks dig the long ball, after all.

But to the owners, what is a home run if there are no RBIs attached to it? Are a lot of home runs good if they're accompanied by a lot of strikeouts? The team requires an all-around solid effort. But to the fan, that's the boring stuff. Fans don't like to pay money to see nothing happen. It's like watching the "Cliff Hangers" game on *The Price is Right* only to find that the yodeler stops one notch before plummeting to his death.

KEY TERMS **pitcher's duel** [pich'erz dool] *n*—a boring game, as in 1-0

The attention span of the fan is essentially a bell curve.

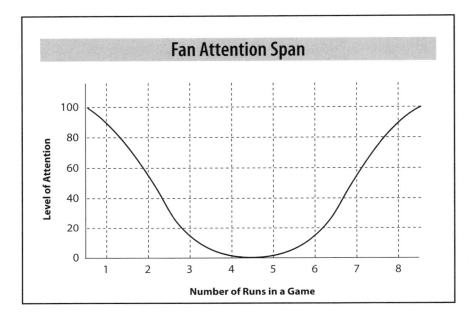

As the curve illustrates, fans enjoy seeing lots of runs scored, but the extreme is also welcomed. If the yodeler were to stay on the mountain yet somehow burst into flames for a historic demise, that's something we would watch. The same can be said for a no-hitter or near no-hitter. Once a team gets one hit, there's a part of your brain associated with memory that shuts down and doesn't slip back into consciousness until an exorbitant number of hits have been accumulated.

KEY TERMS

slugfest [slug'fest] *n*—a game with a football score, as in 17–10

Aside from casual comments that may serve to impress the company you're with, most new stats are basically irrelevant to the fan. That is, unless you are involved in a fantasy league.

Living the Dream

On the off chance that you are unable to secure a position in the Red Sox's front office, you can still run a team. At a relatively low cost, you will be able to purchase professional players and put them into a lineup as you see fit. How can you do this, you ask? Isn't a team expensive?

Yes, but see, you're saving money by consolidating your manager and general manager into one person—you. Plus, you're not paying for a stadium or travel costs. Those are picked up by the players' actual teams. John Henry spent hundreds of millions on his team, while you can spend considerably less. What did his extra cost get him? Well, it gets him better seats at the games and nicer championship rings. But really, that's it. Oh, and he gets a discount on his NESN package.

How is this possible? Fantasy baseball leagues. The stakes? It's all on the line. You will take all the numbers, from batting average to BB/K to complete-game shutouts, and weigh them against salary until you've put together your own living, breathing team of athletes that neither live nor breathe for you (nor know you exist). It's the perfect situation, really. They'd probably be too nervous knowing you were counting on them.

For Those of You Scoring at Home...

Keeping score during a ballgame uses an arcane series of notations that are beyond the scope of our general curriculum. It involves assigning numbers to the players on the field, starting with the pitcher (1) and ending with the right fielder (9), although

FANTASY BASEBALL FAQS

Q What advantages does joining a fantasy baseball league afford me?

A Well, for one, you won't have to spend money on a girlfriend or female companion.

Q What if my player has a game earlier in the day with his real ballclub? Will he be too tired to play for my team later?

A Don't worry, he'll be rested enough to play for you.

Q If a player I have does poorly, am I allowed to bench him from his real team?

A It can't hurt to try. Good luck.

Q I have a chance to attend my own wedding or a fantasy draft in a "keeper league." What should I do?

A The divorce rate is currently hovering around 50 percent; keeper leagues usually last several years. Try to attend both, but if it means leaving the draft before getting a power-hitting infielder, cut ties with your sweetheart.

inexplicably the third baseman is 5 and the shortstop is 6. For more casual fans, one popular in-game activity is keeping track of the pitcher's strikeouts by hanging "Ks" over the outfield wall. Note, however, that one's attire is very important when attempting this type of stat-keeping.

Summary

There are a lot of numbers to deal with for Red Sox fans. It's a whole new world and it's not stopping for the slowpokes. There are many interpretations of each statistic, and those interpretations are different for fans, the press, and the front office.

But get to know your stats. As we mentioned before, baseball is a slow game. There's plenty of time to kill. You might as well kill it with math.

HOW TO SPEAK LIKE A STAT GEEK

Defensive indifference (DI)—when a catcher does not attempt to throw out a base stealer, thus preventing him from being credited with a steal. Now the runner just looks like a charity case and it doesn't help his stats.

Batting average on balls in play (BABIP)—in the event a hitter's batting average is too low, he'll switch over to this statistic, which eliminates strikeouts and foul ball outs in an attempt to raise his average and thus get a larger salary the next time his agent negotiates.

Range factor (RF)—used to determine how much of the field a player can cover. It allows journalists the chance to label him "too slow."

Adjusted ERA (ERA+)—when a pitcher doesn't like his Earned Run Average, he'll hire a crooked statistician to adjust it for him by taking into account the ballpark and league averages.

Groundball-to-flyball ratio (G/F)—this measure is crucial to determining whether a pitcher gives up more ground balls than fly balls.

Gross production average (GPA)—1.8 times on-base percentage plus slugging percentage, divided by four. Duh.

Sabermetrics—a word derived from nerdspeak meaning "statistics."

Wily Mo paradox—the phenomena that causes a player's tape-measure home runs to come before the game begins.

RED SOX

Fun at the Park

Figure out the VORP of two players, taking into account their BABIP, RF, and GPA. Now compare it with the PECOTA of the same players. Which one would you rather have on your team?

Test Your Knowledge

How do you spell relief? Why is it spelled "R-O-L-A-I-D-S?"

Which stats seem made up? Do they really help major league teams make decisions?

What do the numbers (1 4 6 8 9 27 42) on the right-field facade signify?
- (A) the previous night's lotto numbers
- (B) that night's attendance
- (C) the numbers retired by the team
- (D) advertising for the 14892742 Company
- (E) none of the above

60′6″ is:
- (A) the farthest Johnny Damon has ever thrown a ball on the fly
- (B) distance from the pitching rubber to home plate
- (C) the height of former Red Sox first baseman Gary "the Giant" Patterson
- (D) according to court documents, the closest Pedro Martinez can get to Don Zimmer

6

Economics

PREREQUISITE

Must have experience overpaying a scalper for tickets.

LEARNING OBJECTIVES

After reading this chapter, you should be able to:

- Use your scarce resources to meet your competing desires
- Understand why happy people will pay more for tickets
- Describe spending limits and penalties for baseball teams
- List the types of player transactions

The Economy of Baseball

Anyone majoring in economics at most universities is expected to take statistics and calculus, but here at RSU, we waive the calculus requirement (mainly because we don't quite understand it ourselves). Now that you're familiar with statistics and probability, we are able to move from the numbers on the field to the world of off-the-field finance. You'll also learn where the two sets of numbers cross paths.

The production of goods and services (putting a team on the field) and the consumption of those goods (like alcohol) and services (like concession stands that serve alcohol) is what economics is all about. Economics often comes down to the simplest principle around which everything else can revolve—the law of supply and demand.

If You Charge It, Fans Will Pay

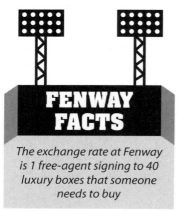

FENWAY FACTS

The exchange rate at Fenway is 1 free-agent signing to 40 luxury boxes that someone needs to buy

People want to go to baseball games. They want to see the Red Sox play. It's the drama and the excitement as much as it is the venue. The Boston Symphony is nice, but you usually know how it's going to end—big crescendo, cymbal smash!—so there's not a whole lot of drama. So Fenway has something to offer and you want it. You want it bad. Exactly how bad do you want it? That's the question.

The members of the Red Sox front office read the newspaper like everyone else and they see fans say things like this in the *Boston Globe:* "I wanted to go [to Fenway] since I was a little girl. I don't really care [how much it costs]. It's just fun to be here. No matter what, this is great.... I can see the [Jumbotron] screen."

Luckily for Larry Lucchino and his wallet, he's the only one who can satisfy that kind of demand.

An Air of Success

What phenomenon, external or internal, compels fans to accept this treatment and pay exorbinant ticket prices? Our willingness comes from a superior standard of living index. This measures the general

Fans reconsider their purchase of the new Lansdowne Street Standing-Room-Only seats.

well-being of a group of people. It is typically a result of a team's GDP (Gross Domestic Pennants). Fans of Kansas City, for example, have been enmeshed in a depression for more than two decades.

The economic activities and success of the team have a powerful impact on the lifestyles and living conditions of the general population. Fans of teams with the highest GDPs typically are happier, enjoy more parades, and have greater baseball-watching opportunities on television. If the team outbids all other teams for the right to sign Daisuke Matsuzaka, that makes the Nation happier. And that will correspond to fans throwing money around, money that they wouldn't have thought to spend if the team was mired in failure. Compare these two Boston franchises between 2003 and 2008:

Measure	Red Sox	Bruins
Number of jerseys sold	4.2 billion (approx.)	42 (approx.)
Consecutive sellouts	486	Define "sellout"
Articles in *Boston Globe*	946, 421	No one makes it to page E12

Spend Reasonably at the Ballpark

Regardless of whether or not you're a thrifty shopper or Charles Barkley at Foxwoods, you should still exercise good judgment when planning an outing at Fenway. You have your own salary cap, so to speak. Every fan should ask themselves, *Should I spend a year's salary on family health care or a day at Fenway?*

You want to enjoy your experience at the ballpark. What you're partaking in is comparable to that once-a-year concert that you don't mind paying through the nose for. Of course, only the best teams will win more than 50 games a year at home. That's 50 out of 81. So your odds of seeing a win are about 60 percent; 40 percent of the time, you end up seeing the equivalent of Paul McCartney with laryngitis or Bruce Springsteen on crutches.

It should be noted that on occasion, you can actually make money off the Red Sox. For example, taking an ordinary David Ortiz jersey and burying it under the new Yankee Stadium can greatly increase its value.

Economic Boundaries

Most sports have a salary cap, including basketball, football, jai alai, and curling. Baseball, however, is not most sports. Baseball is the national pastime. Baseball is America. And America is a capitalist country. Capitalism means the more money, the better.

So baseball teams can spend as much as they want, which is good news for fans of the Red Sox, Yankees, Dodgers, Angels, Cubs, Mets...well, that's about it. However, MLB did create a luxury tax designed to promote competitive balance in the marketplace. The luxury tax penalizes the teams that have the luxury of spending more than the other teams. The other teams are all evidently owned by homeless paupers who unfortunately spent their last hundred million purchasing the team without realizing they needed money for players, too.

Say What?

"Is it 7:05 yet?"—this will show you know when the game starts. It indicates you have your priorities in order. By asking this, you will be required to follow through and drop whatever you're doing at 7:05 in order to find a television to watch the game. Do not ask this during the off-season or when interested in watching a game in another sport.

The Yankees have passed the luxury-tax threshold more often than any other team. They are just trying to destroy the healthy nature of competition, and prefer to simply buy their championships instead of working hard like other franchises through player development and dedication. (There's really no reason to get into the number of times Boston has gone over the line—let's just move along.)

Player Acquisition

So with the rules in place, teams must start acquiring their goods. One of the easiest ways to acquire players is through free agency (although contrary to a popular misconception, free agents are not actually free).

111

PLAYER TO BE NAMED LATER

Many baseball trades involve the Player to be Named Later, yet no one seems to know exactly who he is. Here is an interview with one of baseball's great unknowns:

I'm here with the Player to be Named Later. So, you really haven't been named yet?

That's the question I'm asked the most. My father was away when I was born, so my birth certificate was blank when my mom left the hospital. I guess they never really revisited the issue.

You get traded a lot. Does it get frustrating?

I'd be lying to you if I said it didn't get to me sometimes, but I'm a professional. I just keep my bag packed at all times.

What's the shortest stint you've ever had in a city?

I was actually traded to Montreal along with Carl Pavano in the Pedro Martinez deal, but I never even made it there. I got to the airport and my agent called and said they decided to trade Tony Armas Jr. instead.

You seem pretty optimistic about your lot in life.

Hey, I get to play a game for a living. Do you know how many people would kill to do this? There's not a day that goes by where I don't wake up and tell myself how lucky I am.

So what are your plans for when you decide it's time to hang 'em up?

I've been taking some night classes in the off-season. I'd like to be a financial planner. Maybe finally get a name; make it legal. I'd be ready for something permanent.

KEY TERMS

utility player [ewetill'ittee player] *n*—a player who can play many different positions and fill in on a moment's notice; he also provides the park with gas, water, and electricity

You can build your whole team via free agency if you'd like, but there are no guarantees when it comes to the players you're signing. It's not always just statistics that you must look at. For all the money a team is spending, it might want to know what each player is like on and off the field, in the clubhouse, at the buffet table, etc.

The Red Sox have not always been shrewd shoppers. For example, they spent almost $5 million on Matt Young, a pitcher who couldn't throw the ball to the first baseman, and gave $24 million to Jose Offerman, who was last seen attacking members of the Bridgeport Bluefish with a bat.

Some teams might even decide to hire a private investigator to follow prospective free agents

Oh, Really?

Carl Yastrzemski is tied with Brooks Robinson for the longest tenure with one team in major league history. Yaz was almost traded several times, but the acquiring team had such trouble spelling his name on their uniform that they asked the Red Sox to send another player instead.

around. There are some players who are not big fans of this tactic, however. Mo Vaughn took offense to it and then signed with Anaheim, where he proceeded to fall down the visitor's dugout steps on the first play of his first game with them, badly injuring his ankle. The moral of the story: never sign with Anaheim.

Trades

If you're going to compose a trade for the player of your choice, try to make it as reasonable as possible. A recent study in a trade publication about trades called *All About Trades* showed that 93.7

percent of all trades suggested by fans are ludicrous. General managers are usually wiser than that, but there are also trades made by professional GMs that one might think were proposed by fans. For example, the Red Sox needed a reliever during the 1990 campaign, so they traded for Houston pitcher Larry Andersen. Andersen appeared in 15 games and notched one save before moving on to San Diego. The player Boston traded away, Jeff Bagwell, didn't do much with his career outside of hit 449 home runs and win the 1994 NL MVP Award.

LAST-MINUTE SHOPPING

Teams work feverishly before the trade deadline to improve their roster in time for the stretch run. Here is the timeline of events leading up to Boston's trade of enigmatic slugger Manny Ramirez to the Los Angeles Dodgers in 2008:

July 29, 10:10 AM—Red Sox general manager Theo Epstein calls the general manager in Florida to talk about a time-share for the winter. The subject of Manny Ramirez also comes up.

July 30, 8:06 AM—Theo reads reports from his scouts on Pirates left fielder Jason Bay.

July 30, 8:12 AM—Manny decides on pancakes and waffles for breakfast.

July 30, 8:13 AM—Theo wakes Dodgers general manager Ned Colletti from a deep sleep. "Don't you know there's a time difference?" yells Colletti.

July 30, 8:13 AM—Colletti calls Epstein and says he'll apologize for yelling at Theo if Boston will agree to trade Manny to the Dodgers.

July 30, 1:56 PM—Theo calls the Marlins again with a list of trade alternatives and time-share locations.

July 30, 4:37 PM—Manny hears a rumor he's going to Florida. He rejoices and then pushes down traveling secretary Jack McCormick.

July 30, 5:01 PM—Manny heads into the left-field wall to "use the facilities."

July 30, 5:07 PM—Theo convenes all his baseball people to discuss possible trades.

July 30, 5:55 PM—Manny warms up along the foul line and jokes around with fans. He's seen signing autographs, autographing signs, and signing little children. He pushes the ball boy to the ground.

July 30, 6:39 PM—The buffet table is open to the players in the clubhouse. Manny dogs it to the table and finds there's nothing left but a few stringy fries and some green beans. Manny pushes over the buffet table, which lands on Jack McCormick.

July 31, 8:04 AM—The Red Sox work feverishly on a deal that will both screw them and leave them free of Manny's contract and personality.

July 31, 9:20 AM—Theo revisits his phone call with Pittsburgh regarding Jason Bay. They insist the Dodgers get involved and conference in Colletti, who was sleeping again. He's not happy.

July 31, 3:32 PM—Four Boston sportswriters are seriously injured when they crash into each other trying to get an update on the trade.

July 31, 4:01 PM—The Red Sox announce they acquired Jason Bay while sending Manny to the Dodgers. They also decide to pay the remaining $7 million on Manny's contract because they felt bad over not warning the Dodgers about Grady Little.

Manny Ramirez emerges from the Green Monster to see a game in progress.

Trade Deadline

While speaking of trades, now is a good time to speak of the trade deadline. The trade deadline falls at 4:00 PM EST on July 31. After the July 31 deadline passes, players must pass through waivers before trades can be made. To give you an idea of what passing through waivers is like, imagine an initiation into a fraternity or secret society where you walk between brothers clad in hoods who take turns smacking you with a paddle. Needless to say, players hate being placed on waivers.

Summary

Economics is probably the one subject that comes up the most in administration circles, and it's one that intersects most with the needs of the fans. While the front office must spend money to provide the fans with a product they enjoy, the fans must spend money to support the product, thus replenishing the funds spent by the front office. The fans, on the other hand, are repaid with memories, except for those fans who spend most of their money on alcohol and can't remember what they've seen.

When the off-season comes around and the bell for the free-agency exchange is rung, the team takes everything into account, from their revenue stream to their expenses, to decide how much they'll be able to spend. And if they do outbid all other teams (or themselves) for that high-priced prize, that might mean that you'll be paying more at the ballpark the next year.

RED SOX

Fun at the Park

Go out and buy a baseball team. See how much you can charge people before attendance starts to drop. Fiddle with the prices until you sell out every night and turn a profit.

Test Your Knowledge

Fenway Park : the old Yankee Stadium ::
_____ : _____

(A) Bruce Springsteen : Clay Aiken

(B) Boston : New York

(C) The Chapel : The House that Ruth Built

(D) All of the above

Theo Epstein or Bronson Arroyo—who would you rather have playing guitar at a social function?

John William Henry and John Henry Williams—which one is good and which one was bad? Explain.

How much would you be willing to pay for Red Sox season tickets? Is that more or less than the current value of your 401(k)?

Compare the payroll of the 2008 Red Sox with the 2008 Tampa Bay Rays. Explain how in the world the Sox could lose to them in the 2008 ALCS.

List three places in Fenway Park that could use more advertising.

1. _____

2. _____

3. _____

7

Health

A Machine of Flesh and Bone

You might be asking yourself, *What does health have to do with
Red Sox Nation? You've mentioned our angst, our neuroses, our
culinary habits...Is this mental health? Physical health? What? Tell
me already! I can't take the suspense!*

Are you through? While we are impressed by your passion for acquiring knowledge, it's important not to spiral downward into blubbering impatience.

In addition to focusing on how injuries affect the Red Sox, this chapter will also focus on how the injuries that affect the Red Sox affect *you*. Yes, you run the risk of injury as well. From chapped hands caused by excessive clapping to a bruised molar from biting down into a Cracker Jack only to find an unpopped kernel, you're always putting yourself in a modicum of danger by rooting for the Sox....and that doesn't include the psychological damage.

Putting that knowledge to use, we will then attempt to address any issues you might face as fans. It's a grueling season, both for the players on the field and the fans in their hammocks, listening to the game on their radios. Taking care of yourself is paramount, but your first responsibility is to the team and their players.

$$\frac{\textbf{Inactivity} + \textbf{Sudden Activity}}{\textbf{Age}} = \textbf{Ouchie}$$

Anything can happen in the game of baseball. It's a sport where you stand still for what seems like hours on end and then run at full speed. Other people throw a ball at you as hard as they can. People collide with each other. There's lots of spitting. And you can do this well into your forties these days. Look at knuckleballer Tim Wakefield. His easy delivery and slower-than-slow pitches seem to make him impervious to all the strain injuries of the shoulder and/or arm. But once he reaches 40 years old, his body begins to betray him. An ill-timed sneeze, a particularly potent hiccup, pillow zippers with a vendetta—all can send a player to the disabled list.

The pain might become a blessing in disguise as it can open the doors to myriad endorsement deals. Some players slide more often than they should in an effort to get a raspberry, hoping to become the spokesman for products like Dr. Higgenbacher's Aloe Vera Gel ("The only thing hard enough to take away the pain, but gentle enough to get me sliding again.").

The Commonness of Uncommon Injuries

What could go wrong with a player? A better question is, what couldn't go wrong with a player? Throughout history, major league players have been afflicted with the most ridiculous injuries. Imagine calling into work one day with a pulled eyelid. How would your boss react to that? In the major leagues, you're out for two weeks. An inflamed cuticle? Weeks of rehab. Split ends? Okay, that wouldn't keep you out of anything unless you're a Hollywood movie star, in which case you'd just have your stunt double do the scene.

War of Attrition

Most of the time players "play through the pain," but there are times when they can't. To assume everyone on the Red Sox will be 100 percent all season long is silly. It's your job as a fan not to panic should something happen. (The team is doing enough panicking without you.) If Kevin Youkilis gets hits on the hand by a pitch, they take X-rays of him that night. If J.D. Drew feels

THE WALKING WOUNDED

Here are a few of the injuries some former Red Sox have sustained during their careers:

Wade Boggs—sprained his back removing cowboy boots. That's a big E5.

Bill Lee—jumped into the street to avoid a cat and was hit by a taxi.

Bob Stanley—cut nerves in his pitching hand after falling down the stairs and landing on broken glass while taking out the trash.

David Wells—kicked a bar stool, lost his balance, and fell on a beer glass, cutting his left hand and a tendon in his right wrist.

Roger Clemens—while walking down his driveway to retrieve the newspaper one morning, Roger stumbled and found himself accused of using performance-enhancing drugs.

a twinge in his leg, an MRI is ordered immediately. Heck, if Josh Beckett starts missing the strike zone, an examination by the pitching coach might very well be followed up with a CAT scan. With so much at stake, there's no taking chances.

Your duty as a fan is to let them find out what needs to be found out. If you'd like to go to Mass. General and pace back and forth in the lobby, there's no law against it, but your time would be better served focusing on the next game. However, if Jon Lester misses a start or if Big Papi winces in pain, you might need to check yourself into the hospital for the chest pains you might experience.

Anatomical Anomalies

There are so many parts of the human body that you might not even know you have them. There are some body parts that only athletes, specifically baseball players, seem to injure. That's

Terry Francona breaks the news to David Ortiz that hamate bone injuries are not covered under Boston's health insurance plan.

what makes them professionals. The hamate bone, for instance, is located among a bunch of other small bones in your hand that you don't realize you have. David Ortiz and Dustin Pedroia have both cracked their hamate bones, causing pain while doing hamate-intensive activities such as using their hands.

A Useful Cartilage

Pitchers are often concerned about tearing the labrum. Pitching makes use of your humerus bone (there's nothing funny about the humerus bone), which puts enormous strain on your ball and socket joint (there's nothing funny about balls and sockets either), thus increasing the odds of tearing your labrum (okay, now that sounds kind of funny).

COMMON INJURIES

There are other parts of your anatomy that players also injure frequently:

The "Hammie": The hamstring is the big muscle running up the back of the leg. The cause of it tightening can be a result of not enough stretching on a cold day or a desire to take a few days off to "nurse" it. Left fielders who get paid $20 million a year tend to fall prey to the latter. The "hammie" heals as quickly and mysteriously as it gets injured, but it always remains a concern.

The Cruciate Family: Cruciate and collateral ligaments in the knee hold everything together. Essentially, ligaments are thick fibrous bands connecting bone to bone that can snap as easily as dental floss. There are four—the anterior cruciate ligament, the posterior cruciate ligament, the medial collateral ligament, and the lateral collateral ligament. The ACL is the most commonly injured knee ligament, but it's also so common that it's become easy to repair. Most surgeons now take only a half hour to perform the procedure and complete it using hair pins and a strong adhesive.

The Groin: Guys know what we're talking about when the University announces its commitment to not mentioning the groin. It's too painful to even *think* about hurting.

In the shoulder, the labrum deepens the socket so the ball stays in place. Without a labrum, your arm could escape and go to the country for a long weekend. Players routinely do a labrum count before games just to make sure they're all there.

For a pitcher, no injury is more damaging than one to the most important piece of his arm—the ulnar collateral ligament. This is located in the elbow and it makes it extremely difficult to throw if this ligament is damaged. It will be recommended that you receive Tommy John surgery.

A Bold New World

Tommy John surgery was first performed on Tommy John in 1974 and allowed him to return to the major leagues. This type of surgery is no longer the career-threatening gamble it used to be. In fact, players are getting it earlier and earlier these days, even before they suit up for a major league team. It doesn't seem to hinder them or their chances to get drafted like it once might have.

Take Kristofer Johnson, a 21-year-old out of Wichita State University. The Red Sox selected him as a sandwich pick in the first round of the 2006 draft. And to this day, he's still pitching.

Dr. James Andrews, located in Birmingham, Alabama, is the world's foremost Tommy John-ist. He performs the procedure now with such skill that many times, he does it with his feet, just to show off.

A Savior with a Scalpel

In one of the most dramatic surgeries of all time, Dr. Frank Morgan performed an experimental procedure on that night's starting pitcher before Game 6 during the 2004 ALCS. Morgan used a stapler to repair Curt Schilling's tendon.

In *MacGyver*-like fashion, Morgan needed to work quickly, as the national anthem was being sung. Looking around the room, he spotted some rubbing alcohol, a stapler, and a Montblanc pen. With Schilling on the trainer's table, Morgan told the pitcher to bite down on the fountain pen. Then he felt around for the dislocated tendon, applied the

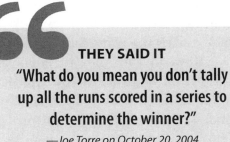

THEY SAID IT

"What do you mean you don't tally up all the runs scored in a series to determine the winner?"
—Joe Torre on October 20, 2004

Oh, Really?

Jason Varitek is the first catcher in major league history to call six no-hitters. He called no-hitters for Pedro Martinez, Hideo Nomo, Derek Lowe, Curt Schilling, Clay Buchholz, and Jon Lester. However, only four are listed in the record books. It's not Jason's fault that Pedro and Curt ruined their respective no-hitters by shaking off Varitek's signs in the ninth inning; Varitek called a no-hitter, those pitchers just didn't throw a no-hitter.

rubbing alcohol, and began to staple (or suture, in doctor lingo) the tendon to the bone. Schilling went out and pitched his heart out that night (Dr. Morgan stapled that back in after the game) and the Red Sox won Game 6, leading them to the rubber match the next night. Although an entire Nation held its collective breath on each pitch, Dr. Morgan never feared because of the mantra that he'd cultivated back in medical school: "Sometimes Home Depot is your best bet for surgical equipment."

A Player's Reputation

When do you consider a player to be injury prone? **Nomar Garciaparra** was injury prone. He missed most of 2001, 2004, 2005, and 2008. Tim Naehring was injury prone. Bill "Injury Prone" Paulsen was probably the most injury-prone player the Red Sox have ever had. An acclaimed shortstop coming out of high school, he was their first pick in one amateur draft back in the 1970s. He sprained his supraspinatus signing his initial contract and never recovered. To this day, he's unable to sign his name with the same flair.

How do you know if a player is playing through pain? If they're playing, you can be sure they're playing through some sort of pain. Bill Mueller played most of his career through pain. He's had 432 knee surgeries, so you figure he's pretty uncomfortable most of the time. Still, he managed to win the AL batting title in 2003. That man was a trooper.

Nomar [no MAAAAAAAAHHHHHHHHH']
n—formerly the best shortstop in the game
until he got traded from Boston, and then he
was less than average

Red Sox manager Terry Francona manages hurt. His knees have been pretty badly damaged over the years and he feels it every time he walks out to the mound to relieve his pitcher. Sometimes he'll send his pitching coach out there, or sometimes he'll just forget the whole thing and let the pitcher "get out of his own damn jam. He's a grown man, after all."

Freak Injuries

The sudden breakdown of one of your favorite players can be a shock to your system as well. For example, when you see Gabe Kapler, a seemingly healthy body with thighs where his biceps should be, running around second base at full speed only to catch a cleat on the turf and tear everything in his knee, that's enough to make you crumple to the ground just as he does. You must keep it together, for his sake and the sake of Red Sox Nation. Be strong. Although Kapler was a fan favorite, save the emotion for when one of your big stars goes down.

You might find that your oblique begins to hurt when Mike Lowell suffers the same injury. Those are called sympathy pains. They are not unusual. You might not even know what an oblique is, but you saw Lowell holding it, so it seizes up on you. You will not have to see a doctor for your sympathy pains, but if it'll make you feel more at ease, go ahead. Just keep in mind that the team needs you, so don't go down. If every fan ended up on the shelf and couldn't make it to the ballpark, there goes the home-field advantage. The team might not want to give it their all with so many empty seats. Just ask the Florida Marlins.

Summary

More than any other sport, baseball players and fans can sustain similar injuries. Sure, football players have more severe injuries, and their fans subject themselves to tailgate-related harm each and every weekend, but no other sport goes from stationary to active so abruptly.

Couple that with the lengthy season and the nature of the game, and there's very little reason to believe anyone will go the whole year without hurting something. So take care of yourself: remember to stretch before cheering, and always keep ointments, bandages, athletic tape, and home remedies at the ready.

Finally, if you feel pain in a part of your body that you didn't know existed, that's probably because one of your favorite players is experiencing the same type of ailment. Either that or you've had a baseball player's body all along. Have your doctor or a local amateur scout check out your hamate bone.

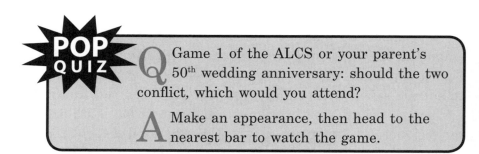

POP QUIZ

Q Game 1 of the ALCS or your parent's 50th wedding anniversary: should the two conflict, which would you attend?

A Make an appearance, then head to the nearest bar to watch the game.

Ask the Valedictorian

How can I perform traditional baseball actions safely?

Hugging: Hugging is fine. The world would be a better place if everyone would just hug. You always see world leaders shake hands after reaching an important understanding. Wouldn't it be nice if they engaged in a little "bring it in" action?

That said, you must observe the intricacies of such platonic affection. The only parts of your body that should touch are hands/upper arms and chest. Anything lower and you're responsible for anything that might happen. A lawyer can't help you.

The choreographed handshake: This depends on the intricacy of the shake. Are feet involved? Will fingers be near eye sockets? Does it involve "copping a feel?" These are questions that you must ask as you plan your movements. Start simple with front of right hands smacking, then back of right hands smacking, then a fist bump, and go from there.

The tushy pat: This works for ballplayers, but not so much for laymen. Imagine if you were at work and handed in a report on time; would a pat on the fanny be an appropriate reward from your boss? It is recommended that high fives, fist bumps, or pats on the back be substituted in place of the tushy pat.

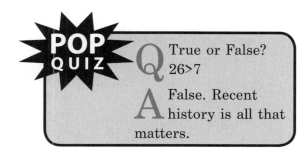

POP QUIZ

Q True or False?
26>7

A False. Recent history is all that matters.

Fun at the Park

Go around to spectators and mention in a concerned tone that their "epidermis is showing." Record their reactions.

Test Your Knowledge

Which bone is not a part of the hand?
(A) lunate
(B) capitate
(C) pisiform
(D) zupcic
(E) scaphoid

What's the worst injury you've ever sustained while attending a baseball game?

Which injuries make you cringe when you see them happen to a member of the Red Sox?

The smell of Ben-Gay—love it or hate it?

8

Literature

Creating Great Art

There are so many great works in the history of our Nation, we can't possibly cover them all here. So this introductory course focuses on the factors that inspired the creation of these works.

Every main character needs a goal. A goal brings conflict. Failure to reach that goal brings drama. Tales pertaining to the Red Sox are brimming with these important elements. The team has been fraught with drama for the majority of its existence.

Red Sox fans write of themes important to them. When they pick up their pens or sit at their computers, those themes invariably include disappointment, bullies, failure, heartbreak, unrequited love, public displays of drunkenness, the power of belief, and the loss of innocence.

Since victory has been achieved recently, you, the new class of writers, will likely utilize decidedly more optimistic themes: redemption, celebration, success, maturity, reciprocated love, public displays of drunkenness, and the power of prayer.

But how does our writing differ from that of the Cubs fan? In essence, Cubs fans lack the drama much of the time. Sure, there was 1969, Leon Durham's misplayed ball in 1984, and Steve Bartman in 2003; those incidents worked for plot, but none of their front-office employees has ever had to escape the building in a gorilla suit. Events about which to write are few and far between.

The Master of Horror

Now let us take a look at the works of one of our Nation's literary giants—Stephen King. As a lifelong Red Sox fan, he's had plenty of material from which to cull.

KEY TERMS

wasted [way'sted] *adj.*—totally intoxicated, inebriated, pissed, blitzed, smashed, hammered, obliterated, liquored up, plastered, Newcastled, sloshed, tanked, trashed, wrecked; drunk

King's stories overflow with the goriest details, describing supernatural evil lurking just below the surface. Need we explain how his genre corresponds to the Red Sox?

In 1975, the Red Sox's loss to the Big Red Machine moved him to write *The Shining*. In 1985, King wrote a poem titled "Paranoid: A Chant" for his *Skeleton Crew* anthology. It was a diary, written in first-person, of a paranoid, superstitious person who complains of persecution. The victim thinks his enemies are part of a massive government conspiracy. A paranoid, superstitious person concerned that the world is conspiring against him? Does that remind you of someone you know, or perhaps, *everyone* you know?

But it wasn't until 1986's *It* that King bared his soul for all to see. After the pain of 1975, 1978, and now 1986, he compared liking the team to a malevolent, shape-shifting, child-killing monster that lurks in sewers and storm-drains and takes on the shape of children's biggest fears.

It took a lot out of the author and that is why he only wrote cheery horror

HOT STOVE READING LIST

Of Mice and Manny

Catcher in the Bullpen

Interview with an Umpire

One Flew over the Monster Seats

Death of a Season

The Brothers Conigliaro

Lord of the World Series Rings

Hunt for Red Sox October

stories unrelated to any baseball team after that.

In 1999, he wrote *The Girl Who Loved Tom Gordon,* which actually had nothing to do with the Red Sox or their former closer Tom Gordon. Finally, in 2004, King reexamined his allegiance to the Red Sox along with his friend and fellow author Stewart O'Nan in the critically acclaimed supernatural thriller *Faithful,* which was subsequently adapted into *Fever Pitch,* a film starring Jim Rice and Dennis Eckersley.

With the recent successes of the Red Sox, King has been able to purge his frustrations and has sought happier experiences in his life for inspiration. He's currently working on a children's

Ask the Valedictorian

Should fans ever renounce their allegiance to the Red Sox?

Renouncing your allegiance is a serious decision and should not be taken lightly. If you decide that you've had enough and no longer wish to root for the Red Sox, simply go to any local Boston bar, find a bartender, and order a half-dozen beers. When you feel ready, stand up on a chair or barstool and formally forsake your commitment to the team. Your speech should be brief but heartfelt. For example:

"I can't take it anymore. They're ruining my life. They suck! They're not going anywhere and anyone who thinks differently is insane. From this day forward, I am no longer a Red Sox fan…I'm serious…I mean it…They are dead to me."

Then pass out on the ground. When you come to, simply pick yourself off the floor and go on with your life. Then, around late March or April, you will revert back to being a Red Sox fan. Sorry.

Stephen King, the master of horror and suspense, notices a classified ad for a used snowblower.

Christmas book. In it, Santa Claus waits until all the little boys and girls are asleep, lands with nary a clatter on their roofs, slides quietly down their chimneys, and unleashes unspeakable horror on the families. It's supposedly based on a true story.

That's what happens when there's no more sadness in an artist's heart.

Oh, Really?

The Red Sox came one strike away from winning the World Series in every year that Dwight Evans hit the first pitch of the season out of the park for a home run.

Poetry

We conclude this section by looking at some of our most famous poems. Each poet demonstrates the feelings of the Nation as if written from the collective mindset.

A Limerick
(1967)

I once had an Impossible Dream
The details made Boston cheer and scream
Lonborg and Yaz had a Cy and Crown
But in the end, it still led to a frown
For Babe had put a curse on our team.

A Haiku
(1978)

Bucky Bleepin' Dent
Damn you, Bucky Bleepin' Dent
Your bat was corked. Bleep!

The Curse
(2004)

Ah, so it was during that October when our ballclub got rocked
over
In a scenario we'd seen many times before
Yet again we'd need a hero, beaten badly down 3-0
I drained my beer, though, all alone a'front the store
And thought of what the future held in store
Still painful now and evermore

And their fans began the bragging as our hopes had started
  sagging
Their constant dirty ragging is what I, frankly, most abhor
They think they're clever when they speak wisely almost never
Their constant endeavor is to make us Sox fans feel insecure
Each time they said it, it'd make us feel sore
They'd say the year and nothing more
The more I pondered, the more it clear, for us to wait til next
  year
Then the ninth, it did appear with us behind in the score.
But I had a feeling that Roberts' mastered stealing
Would send Rivera reeling, shaking the foundation of his lore
We found the chink in the their closer's armor and won Game
  Four.
Now my heart was timidly beating as their lead was surely
  fleeting
This, the umpteenth meeting, could end better than those we've
  seen before.
I found myself grinning as another game in extra innings
After they had been winning and again failed to close the door.
Big Papi swung and won once more
Twice in one day was his encore
Still the straits were dire, from such excitement I never tire
Coming down to the wire, the series looked not like a bore.
And Schilling's fabled pitching, with his splitter so bewitching
His bloodied tendon valiantly twitching—truly heroic to his core
To see their lead gone made their chins scrape on the floor.
Now it came down to but one more.
So the battle's tied up as their brittle bats had dried up
What a wild ride, huh? Better than the days of yore.
The one that we call "Jesus" after batting unseemly grievous
Hit the ball out twice to please us allowing us to win the war.
And so their fans must quoth the Babe, nevermore

Quoth the Babe, "nevermore."
The Yankees, beaten and lost, while down in Hell, they had a
　　frost,
Boston fans became sauced, a smile on the face of depressed
　　Eeyore.
But still a reason to be leery as ahead lay one more Series
Though our eyes were red and bleary from the pride on hearts
　　we wore
If we win this, no one could chant "Nineteen-Eighteen"
　　evermore.
They'd not chant "Nineteen-Eighteen" evermore.
And so it was against the Cards with our city packed with
　　guards
Many balls had left the yard making victory seem secure
So at 11:40 on our clocks when the last batter left the box
Then the Boston Red Sox were the champs of 2004
And they must chant "Nineteen-Eighteen" nevermore.
Chant "Nineteen-Eighteen" nevermore.

The Pap in the Cap
(2007)
[Excerpt]

We looked
Then we saw him come in like a zap
We looked
And we saw him
The Pap in the Cap
And he said to us
"Why do you sit with gloom on your face?
I know it's 3–1
And the runs are not running
Give us a chance

And the guns will start gunning."
"I know what will make you feel fine,"
Said the Pap.
"I know these new pitches,"
said the Pap in the Cap.
"A lot of great ones.
I will show them to you
The Tribe
Will not mind at all if I do."
But the Indians said, "No! No!
Make the Pap go away
Tell that Pap in the cap
We do not want to play."
Then we saw him rear back
And throw them the heat
He tossed a slider, then glider,
And the batters took a seat.
And a curve and the splitter
And the 2- and 4-seamer
And the slider and the slutter
And heat as fast as a "Beemer."

Summary

The feelings that can be put into words by these masters, as well as by the next generation of Red Sox writers, and the feelings that those words evoke from the reader, is almost magical. And it all sprung from the doings of the Boston Red Sox.

Each and every moment, each and every person, each and every sight and sound has a story in it. Some end in sadness and some end with jubilation. The constant activity surrounding the Red Sox provides the constant lifeblood of art. The only thing left to do is to tap it.

Fun at the Park

Write a book about the Red Sox. Get it published. Become famous and make lots of money. Throw out the first pitch at Fenway.

Test Your Knowledge

What emotions did the sample poems ignite in you?

Which Stephen King story makes you think of the Red Sox?

What the heck is a *sonnet*?

Reading Comprehension

The din of the fancy restaurant became more dominant as silence gripped the table. Ron looked pensive. He did not blink as he pondered the situation. This was a rare moment in which he did not know how to react.

"Ron? Ron?"

He snapped out of it as his fiancée's voice pierced his eardrums. He lowered his gaze slightly and retrained his focus, this time on her face. "Yes, dear?"

Continued on next page

"We were talking about potential dates for our wedding," said Diane, tapping her finger on the table to keep her anger in check.

"Uh-huh." Ron's attempt at feigning interest fell woefully short as his eyes floated off center again, staring into the distance.

This time, Diane followed his line of sight and whipped her head around toward the bar, where she saw a television sitting on a shelf right next to the high-end alcohol. "You're watching the game, aren't you?"

"What? The game? No! There's a game on?" Ron said.

"You didn't hear a word I said," she challenged.

"No, sweetums, I was listening intently. And then I saw the Sox throw a wild pitch and a run scored. I think the sudden movement on the screen must've caught my attention. I just zoned out for a second."

Diane stood, judging him, weighing her options and his future on her imaginary scales. Ron held his breath. He managed a sycophantic smile. After a long beat, Diane acquiesced, "Fine." This prompted an exhalation from Ron that seemed to last several minutes. "So what do you think?" she quickly followed up.

"I don't think he should even be in the game. He's been throwing junk all season and you put him in with the score tied and runners on? Are you crazy? Why he wasn't sent down to Triple A if not released completely is insane. I would really—"

"About our wedding!" she interrupted.

Ron jumped. "Oh, right."

Continued on next page

Continued from previous page

1. Ron is most likely what type of fan?
   (A) Idiot
   (B) Rising Son
   (C) Dirt Dog
   (D) GM
   (E) Ostrich

2. In Ron's eyes, who was to blame for the wild pitch?
   (A) Diane
   (B) The manager
   (C) God
   (D) Himself
   (E) The general manager

3. For what month was Ron and Diane's wedding planned?
   (A) The first month after Ron had his head removed
       from his butt
   (B) October
   (C) March
   (D) They eloped in a place with no TV/radio/Internet
       access
   (E) None of the above

9

Philosophy

PREREQUISITE

A desire to know if knowing means you exist.

LEARNING OBJECTIVES

After reading this chapter, you should be able to:

- Understand why Red Sox fans think the way they do
- Recognize our philosophical ancestors
- Explain the truth about truth
- Comprehend ethics

Philosophy is generally regarded as a graduate-level program here at the University, but it plays such an important role in understanding Red Sox fans and their loyalties that the head of the philosophy department lobbied to have a general overview of the subject made part of the core curriculum. On the plus side, grading is very lenient, because if you get a "C" on top of your paper, how do you know it's really there?

Deep-Seated Feelings

It is natural for a fan of Boston's baseball nine to embrace a philosophical approach to life. Why, after all the heartache, did we stand by our boys through thick and thicker? Yes, it eventually paid off, but did we know that it would with absolute certainty? For example, if the sun rises every day for a year (let alone 86 years), you have no reason to expect it not to rise the following morning. But Red Sox fans kept believing that the Red Sox would win—that one day the sun would *not* rise. It's the same reason we watch Game 6 on ESPN Classic hoping that Calvin Schiraldi will strike out Gary Carter to end the game.

Our Philosophical Ancestors

Socrates, Plato, and Aristotle have all had an impact on Red Sox Nation in one way or another, though many years earlier. Each mused differently on subjects including life, purpose, and the benefits of going to your closer in the eighth inning should the situation dictate.

Socrates

Socrates (Or "Soc" as he was known by his friends) was most certainly destined to become a Red Sox fan and thus, in matters of philosophy, is our guardian and patron saint. How could it be thought otherwise since he killed himself after one of the chariot teams he followed blew a 14-game lead in late Sextilis?

Before Socrates, philosophers did not believe gods or supernatural forces caused natural events like a ball bending perfectly off the pole during Game 6 of the 1975 World Series. Now we know other forces are constantly at work...or are they?

Soc wasn't known as much for his doctrines as he was for his method...his method for coming up with doctrines. The Socratic

Method consisted of asking a question and allowing people confident of their answers to answer it. Back then, he would ask one question and follow it up with, "How do you know?" or "What do you mean?" To this day, the Boston media uses such tactics.

But as we mentioned, for all his insight, Soc was still traumatized by the Athenian team's lack of chemistry (one reporter summed up the lack of camaraderie by saying, "11 players, 11 chariots."). He was constantly hounded by the thought, *If only they had a good manager*.... No amount of thinking could undo that.

Plato

Plato attempted to identify the nature of a philosophically important notion by defining it. What is justice? What is pain? He clearly showed signs of being destined for Red Sox fandom. He also reasoned that ordinary things change, but their forms do not. A loss can be by one run or 10 runs, but either is still accompanied by a long, depressing winter.

Understanding the soul was a goal of Plato's. He believed that the body dies and disintegrates while the soul continues to live forever, existing without a body, sometimes going out for Greek food and neglecting to leave a tip. Then it gets reincarnated in another body and returns to the world, retaining a dim recollection of the past.

Plato would have argued that Red Sox fans have experienced all of their ancestors' pain and suffering, even in their few years on earth. It sure seems like he's right; even during your first game at Fenway, you'll feel connected to every fan and every player since the Americans came to town. Consider this: how many of you produced 86 years' worth of tears on October 27, 2004?

Aristotle

Before there was A-Rod, there was A-Rot. Aristotle entered Plato's school when he was 18 and remained there for 20 years. A lifetime student? Overeducated? Now, if that doesn't qualify someone to be a Red Sox fan, what does?

Aristotle wrote tirelessly and divided his writings into three groups: popular writings, memoranda and statistics, and dirty limericks (he had a bit of a naughty side). In his popular writings, he would criticize the local charioteers and their pit crews for the crappy job they were doing. He gained quite a following with his biting wit and pop-culture references. His peers referred to him as "the Sports Gvy" because they didn't have the letter *u* yet.

Aristotle was big into the gladiator thing. He compiled data that he felt would give competitors an advantage over their opponents, but not many gladiators used his information. They preferred to go with their guts, which Aristotle found ironic because it was usually their guts that they left on the amphitheatre floor when they failed to heed his advice. Bill James is a clear disciple of Artistotle's scientific passions.

146

Aristotle's Gladiator Projections			
Gladiator Info	vs. lefties	vs. lions	vs. righties
Taller than 5'10"	.627	.031	.450
Practicing Catholics	.390	.006	.511
Barefoot fighters	.300	.019	.277
Allergic to feta cheese	.248	.000 (0 for 17)	.800

What does all this have to do with our philosophical values as Red Sox fans? Well, Aristotle believed that all things in nature have some purpose, even 8:00 PM start times. Stoics, on the other hand, believed that all things are fated to be. This was a strict determinist way of thinking and seems to fit in with the divide we possess amongst ourselves today.

We Panic, Therefore We Are

In delving into metaphysics, we must first ask, "Do the Red Sox exist?" Your answer might be, "If they don't, then I've been losing sleep for nothing." But the correct answer is reached through the logical statement, "They leave too many men on base, therefore, they are."

But it's the follow-up questions that may infuriate you—how do you know they left men on base? What is real? Is a curveball real? Does it break from 12-to-6 or does the ground below break from 6-to-12, giving the batter the perception that he's going to be called out on strikes? Either way, sign that pitcher to a multiyear deal and hope he develops a second out-pitch to make the deuce even more devastating.

Is it real when Terry Francona brings in a pitcher who blows the game for the Red Sox or did the other team win the

Oh, Really?

Mike Greenwell earned the AL MVP Award in 1988. Unfortunately, the rules said only steroid users were eligible for the award, so the honor went to Jose Canseco.

game independent of Francona's move? The appearance of failure or a lack of success fuels our thoughts.

That scoots us right along to the concept of **free will**. Do we possess free will or are our actions determined by causes over which we have no control? The manager should have known that the batter would be expecting a first-pitch slider and, therefore, should never have put that particular reliever in, nor should he have allowed the slider be the pitch of choice. It's obvious, right?

Yeah, sure, whatever you say. Anyway, here are four metaphysical theories that you can choose from in making your argument to the manager.

Materialism

Only matter has real existence; feelings, thoughts, and other mental phenomena are produced by the activity of matter.

In other words, "Matter made us hate the manager!"

This is the simplest of the four concepts. It might not hold water, but it certainly gives you a scapegoat for your feelings so you don't have to qualify them to anyone.

Idealism

Plato was into this. (He was also into mooning people in the Parthenon, so take it with a grain of salt.) He taught that only

KEY TERMS

free will [free will] *n*—a philosophical concept that believes anyone who hurls themselves into the harbor does so of their own volition

ideas are real and that all other things only reflect those ideas. In other words, every material thing is an idea or a form of an idea; mental phenomena are what are fundamentally important and real.

There are very few people in Red Sox Nation who think this way. Perhaps in Anaheim, where the sun shines all the time and they cheer when a monkey tells them to, but not here.

Imagine if we all focused idealistically. We'd all imagine that the Red Sox have won more World Series than the Yankees. Heck, we'd probably imagine that Yankees fans were only three feet tall with their hands sewn to their hips. In fact, just for a moment, put the book down and imagine that. If enough people attend RSU, perhaps we can change reality.

Idealism is a great concept, it just takes too much coordination. It's hard enough to get the wave to go all the way around a ballpark once. If we could get together on idealism, it would take the worry away. But wouldn't that be boring? Also, after imagining winning, you'd have to imagine celebration parades through the city. Plus, if you're going to imagine the Sox winning, you might as well imagine the Patriots, Celtics, Bruins, and Revolution raising banners, too. Then Government Center would be overpacked with all those victory speeches. You'd have an imaginary logistical nightmare that the imaginary city planning board would not want to deal with.

Mechanism

Mechanism says that all happenings result from purely mechanical forces and not from purpose; thus, the universe has no purpose. It's like an ocean without a dolphin. Get it? No porpoise. (Note: the University discourages undergraduates from making marine puns of any kind.)

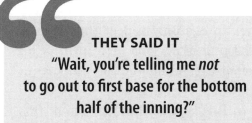

Anyway, it's hard to get behind mechanism as a Sox fan. Put benefit of the doubt behind you and you're forced to believe that the umpires were actually blind during the 1999 ALCS against the Yankees and legitimately blew all those calls. It had nothing to do with a payoff from Steinbrenner or their fear of getting out of Yankee Stadium alive had they ruled against the home team, nor did it pertain to a concerted effort by the powers that be to boost the World Series ratings by promoting the New York team over the Boston team as the materialists might have you believe.

Nope, a mechanist would say it was just a collective group of blind umpires who got their jobs because the aptitude tests they took weren't stringent enough. There was no curse and the fates did not "deem it so." What fun is that?

Teleology

A teleologist believes the universe and everything in it exists and occurs for some purpose. In other words, "It is obvious that the Red Sox exist only to torment us."

This is a good one to get behind. It's quick and to the point. But if you want to find another purpose, go right ahead. You don't have to be married to the idea of torment.

The Blame Game

Even thinking metaphysically leaves us curious and without any definitive answers. The question most Red Sox fans find themselves asking is, "Who is to blame?"

Was it Bill Buckner's fault even though Game 6 was already tied up when the ball squirted through his legs? Was Tim Wakefield to blame for giving up the final run of the 2003 ALCS? Did Mike Torrez deserve to be stuck with voodoo pins after losing the one-game playoff in 1978? That is where philosophies diverge.

Using Knowledge to Point the Finger

Red Sox fans are, first and foremost, knowledgeable. (Second and not-quite-as foremost, they are passionate, drunk, and occasionally sloppy.) We'll delve into epistemology briefly and look at the various ways of knowing, the nature of truth, and the relationship between knowledge and belief.

There are two types of knowledge, priori and empirical.

We can acquire priori knowledge by knowing that there are nine players on the field at one time, 25 players on the major league roster, and 40 on the 40-man roster, so we can reason that the Red Sox won't be carrying a third catcher during the playoffs. (No experience is needed to come to that conclusion. It's just common sense.)

Empirical knowledge, on the other hand, is attained from observation and experience. Knowing Trot Nixon couldn't hit lefties was learned by watching him try to hit lefties. And unless he's asked to do so against your team in, say, the eleventh inning of a League Championship Series, you can be pretty sure that he won't hit lefties.

It poses a great philosophical dilemma. Using knowledge that is reasoned and knowledge that is observed, who is to blame?

THEY SAID IT
"We've got a 14½-game lead in *August,* fer cryin' out loud! There's no way we're gonna blow it."
—*Anonymous fan in 1978*

The options are the manager, the general manager, individual players, or the other team.

Everyone Blew It

Let's take this example: a pitcher gives up a line drive up the middle in the seventh inning of a tie game. It proves to be the winning run.

If the manager leaves a pitcher in and that pitcher loses, the manager left the pitcher in too long. If the manager pulls a pitcher and allows a relief pitcher to lose the game, why in the great name of Dwight Evans' arm did he pull that pitcher? He can't win.

Oh, Really?

Spinoza once said, "If a tree falls in the forest and no one is there to hear it, do the Yankees gain a half-game?"

The general manager is the one who didn't acquire the horses needed to pull the carriage. So what if the pitcher has done consistently well throughout the season and then had an off day? The man needed to sign a pitcher who can do well in that particular situation against that particular lineup *every* day.

The players? They suck. These pitchers have gotten strikeouts before. Why did they fail to do so in that situation? But maybe it's not their fault. They never should have been in the game in the first place (see: manager). In fact, they never should have been on the team in the first place (see: general manager).

Or is the true culprit the other team? No. We cannot lay blame across the dugout steps of the

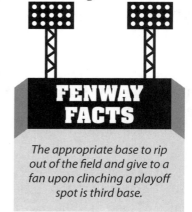

FENWAY FACTS

The appropriate base to rip out of the field and give to a fan upon clinching a playoff spot is third base.

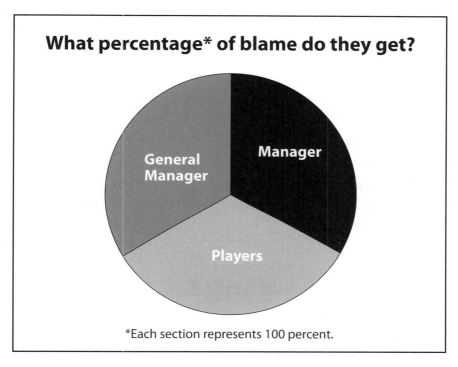

What percentage* of blame do they get?

General Manager

Manager

Players

*Each section represents 100 percent.

other team. They have never beaten the Red Sox. This cannot be stressed enough. It is not by the play of their opponents that the Red Sox ended up on the short end of the stick. It is merely through some fault of our own (see: manager, general manager, or players).

An Endless Struggle for Truth

What is truth, and how can we know what is true and false? We'll use the word "true" for ideas that we find congenial and we want to believe. "We would have won the game had it not been raining." (Or in the case of the Yankees, "had the bugs not adhered themselves to our set-up man, he would have mowed those Indians down.") The problem is that many people, even throughout a similar fan base, disagree with some of those "true" beliefs.

How can we, as a group, get to the actual true ideas? We can use a variety of theories: correspondence theory, pragmatic theory, skepticism, and coherence theory.

Correspondence Theory

An idea is true if it corresponds to the facts or reality. This really sucks the wind out of your sails on that whole "coulda woulda shoulda" argument. It does give credence to those jerks who say, "If the Sox were better, they might have actually won more." Losers.

Pragmatic Theory

An idea is true if it works with or settles the problem it deals with. Sounds good, doesn't it?

Fan: What is wrong with Mike Timlin?

Pragmatist: Oh, nothing. He simply didn't get any good calls from the umpire.

End of story. The problem with Timlin's ineffectiveness has been projected onto the umpire.

Skepticism

You'd think by the name alone that this is what we Red Sox fans hang our hat on. Skepticism states that knowledge is impossible to attain and truth is unknowable. So we don't know what happened out there, but we do know we lost. Now where's the fun in that?

Coherence Theory

Truth is a matter of degree, and any idea is true to the extent it fits together with other ideas that one holds. Looks like we have a winner: we believe what we want to believe. It all makes sense now.

You were exactly right when you thought that the networks wanted the other team to win to boost ratings or to promote parity, or that the owner bought off the umps. That's not too hard to fathom since the ice was broken in the NBA by Tim Donaghy.

Just fit the pieces that are floating around with your argument, but don't contradict yourself, and for goodness sake, don't ramble unintelligibly. It's not called incoherence theory, after all.

Our Ethics

What is good and what is bad? This is the quintessential question all members of our society must confront. Although usually a road uniform–colored gray area, the perk of being a Red Sox fan is that right and wrong are mostly black and white: the Yankees, pinstripes, and forcing players to be clean shaven is wrong; everything else is right. Got it?

However, to jump to such conclusions without fair consideration is downright, well, Yankee-like. Hence, we look at the question in three different ways.

Relativism

What is wrong depends on the particular culture involved, so no basic standards exist by which a culture may be judged right or wrong. Yankees fans will try to hide behind this manner of reasoning. They see the opposite of what we see because they see their culture as better than ours.

How narrow-minded can one be? We're the ones who are better. Of course, they're wrong, so who cares what they think? Let's skip right over this.

Objectivism

There are objective standards of right and wrong that can be discovered and that apply to everyone. This is the manner of thinking that is followed by the other 28 teams in the league. They might say that Red Sox fans are similar to Yankees fans, however (a) they are being subjective, and (b) who cares what they think?

Subjectivism

All moral standards are subjective matters of taste and opinion. This is more for the "live and let live" crowd. No thank you. We Sox fans will stick with objectivism, if you don't mind. Besides, who cares what they think?

So what makes actions right and wrong? A crazy fan dives into the net behind home plate at Yankee Stadium. (Wrong!) Someone takes a swipe at Gary Sheffield as the right fielder attempts to field a ball against the wall at Fenway. (Hey, seemed like the fan was just going for the ball.) A Yankee fan throws a pretzel with mustard on it at a visiting team's fans. (Wrong!) A Red Sox fan throws a slice of pizza at another Red Sox fan. (Hey, they were both Red Sox fans.)

So there you have it.

Turning Your Mind Inside Out

Now that you've formed your opinions based on facts and observations, turn your linear compass from the direction that it's on—what *did* happen—to what *could* happen.

For example, you might believe Jason Varitek will hit a weak grounder to the right side. Based on the fact that he's been doing that all season (empirical knowledge), we can assume truth. But there are ways to see this truth with optimism; let go of your negativity for a moment. Look at it this way: since there's nobody on base, he will not hit into a double play. It's this optimism that propels us into a different state. Yes, he'll still ground weakly to second, but he cannot possibly hit into a double play. Hey, it's a start. And then you can work your way up to believing that the Sox, after enduring a devastating five-game losing streak, will not lose the following day. True, it's their off day, but again, it's a start. Baby steps!

Philosophies of the Far East

A more detailed look at philosophy delves into schools of thought from the Far East, which focus on six-man pitching rotations, no pitch counts, and posting fees. This will be studied in graduate-level classes, but for now, you're all set when it comes to what philosophies inhabit the dark and cavernous minds of Red Sox fans.

Summary

The mind of the Red Sox fan is an active one, filled with philosophical concepts they can hide behind or be empowered by. We understand where most of the blame ends up and how it can be rationalized. One might not be right, but does one even know that one exists?

RED SOX

Fun at the Park

Several Red Sox players, past or present, have the same names as Massachusetts towns. Name them. (Hint: Daryl Boston never played for the Red Sox. Neither did Sam Provincetown.)

Test Your Knowledge

How does a "half-game" exist in time and space? If the Red Sox are up 4½ games on the Yankees, is one of them in another dimension?

Barry Bonds is . . .
- (A) great
- (B) the best HR hitter of all time
- (C) an absolute moron
- (D) in for a world of pain when the flaxseed oil wears off
- (E) roid-tastic!!!

What is Snodgrass' muff?
- (A) An infamous blunder in the 1912 World Series
- (B) The mitten worn by Fred Snodgrass in place of a baseball glove
- (C) None of the above
- (D) All of the above

10

Religion

You don't have to be a religious person to like the Red Sox, but if you do like the Red Sox, you are most definitely religious. The team emits a piety not seen in most religions. We call the ballpark "the Chapel," we wear sacramental garments, and we spend much of our time in prayer (we may not face east when we do, but that's only because we have no idea which direction is east thanks to the geniuses who laid out our city).

What kind of a religion unites us? Call it passion, call it spirituality, call it too much free time on our hands—the Red Sox are sacred to all of us. So how have we distilled our feelings into a religion?

Soxism: A Religion All its Own

The majority of those living in Red Sox Nation are of the same belief—Soxism. The rest are agnostic or Jewish.

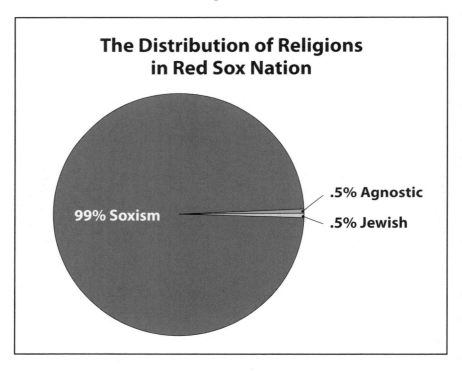

The Distribution of Religions in Red Sox Nation

99% Soxism

.5% Agnostic

.5% Jewish

The religion was founded along the Judeo-Christian belief of cheer unto others as you would have them cheer unto you. There is no separation of church and state here, which is the main difference between Red Sox Nation and the United States of America (that, and we can't declare war if we want oil reserves).

In that sense, Boston is the Vatican City of American professional sports. Rules installed by the team are adopted by all their zealots; a decree to wear red at the ballpark will be followed by most practitioners.

Early Beginnings

The founder of our religion was a man named "Nuf Ced" McGreevey, the patron saint of passionate fans. McGreevey was a tavern owner who preached from the gospel of Guinness ("Brilliant!") and people listened until they passed out. In the early 1900s, he spoke of this new team in town, the Pilgrims, and the joy they would bring. Lives would be changed, priorities altered, and perceptions molded.

McGreevey was prone to visions. He would say, "I see you ordering another round," and you did. "I see us going to Pittsburgh," and he was right. (This is where the term *pilgrimage* came from.)

His prophecies became legendary,

which brought more and more followers to his bar. And patrons knew he spoke the truth because he punctuated it with the phrase, "'Nuf ced," which is pretty profound, even for those times. It wasn't open for debate, plus most patrons couldn't see straight enough to argue.

Let's examine several different sects—fair-weathah (reform), supahfans (conservative), and wicked fanatical (orthodox).

Fair-Weathah

These fans only pay attention during the high holidays, including Patriots Day, division-clinching games, and games against the Yankees. They eat whatever they want at the ballpark, they don't know all the hymns, nor when to yell "So good! So good! So good!" during "Sweet Caroline," they rarely pay for tickets, opting instead to only attend a game on someone else's dime, and they would consider rooting for the underdog even if that means the Tampa Bay Rays.

Supahfans

Their customs include sitting in the same seat during a rally, not mentioning a win before its time, and wearing official Red Sox undergarments. They are strict with their diet, eating only sausages or hot dogs at the ballpark and never fruit cups or chicken Caesar salad wraps.

Wicked Fanatical

These pictures of extreme fandom are always praying, take holidays after a Red Sox loss, can't be seen out of the house without proper clothing, and only allow other Sox fans into their homes, where they have a picture of Ted Williams overlooking each room.

KEY TERMS **the Chapel** [fen'way pahk] *n*—a place where zealots and non-zealots alike come to pray

They name their pets and/or children after Red Sox players or Fenway Park, quit any job that requires them to miss games, and never accept calls until after the game is over.

Religious Rites and Ceremonies

Acts of worship reinforce the moral and cultural commitments and understandings of the community. Our worship as a group proves our commitment to the Red Sox. It breaks down to individuals worshipping together. Most of the time, it's a personal act that is duplicated by everyone else simultaneously. Personal worship, whether public or private, is often aided by the observance of disciplines and techniques that focus the attention of the worshipper upon the sacred or holy. That could be in the form of silence, devotional readings, prayers, a wave, music, works of art, or banners with "Dice-K" written on them.

First, we must know what the unimpeachable rules are.

The Chapel

Fenway Park, also known as "the Chapel," is our house of worship. Though the structure is relatively new, its location is more than

KEY TERMS **wicked** [wick'id] *adv.*—really, very, a heckuva lot, more than you could ever imagine

The 10 Fenway Commandments

[reprinted with permission from Sarah Green,
as appeared in Further Fenway Fiction *(Rounder Books, 2007)]*

Hear, O Fenway Faithful, the statutes and judgments which I speak in your ears this day, that ye may learn them, and keep, and do them.

I am the Team thy Red Sox, which have brought thee out of the Curse of the Bambino, out of the house of bondage.

1. Thou shalt have no other Teams before me.

2. Thou shalt not buy unto thee any other team's graven merchandise, or any bobblehead of any player that is in Canada above, or that is in the States below, or that is in the States to the West: Thou shalt not bow down thyself to them, nor root for them: for I the Team thy Red Sox am a jealous Team, visiting the iniquity of the fathers upon the children unto the third and fourth generation of them that hate me (or them that selleth players to finance Broadway musicals); And showing mercy unto thousands of them that root for me, and keep my commandments.

3. Thou shalt not jeer the name of the Team thy Red Sox in vain; but the Team shall hold him guiltless that cheereth and maketh a joyful noise unto the Team.

4. Remember the season, to keep it holy. Two-hundred and three days shalt thou labor, and do all thy work: But one-hundred and sixty-two days are the game days of the Team thy Red Sox: in them thou shalt not do any work, thou, nor thy son, nor thy daughter, thy assistant, nor thy cleaning lady, nor thy dog, nor thy cat, nor any of thy gold-fish, nor thy stranger that is within thy cul-de-sac: For in the off-season, the Team made offense and defense, the pitching rotation, and all that in them is, and played the season: wherefore the Team blessed the season, and hallowed it.

5. Honor thy hot dog vendor and thy beer man, as the Team thy Red Sox hath commanded thee; that thy season may be prolonged, and that it may go well in October, in the Fenway which the Team thy Red Sox giveth thee.

6. Thou shalt not kill for season tickets.

7. Thou shalt not have pennant fever for two teams at once.

8. Thou shalt not steal away from thy seat until the final out hath been recorded. It is easier for a camel to pass through the eye of a needle than for a businessman to stay nine innings on Opening Day.

9. Thou shalt not bear false witness against thy umpire. Let them alone: they be blind leaders of the blind. And if the blind lead the blind, both shall fall into the dugout.

10. Thou shalt not covet the Yankees' stadium, thou shalt not covet the Yankees' payroll, nor their farm system, nor their manager, nor their free agents, nor their Championship rings, nor anything that is the Yankees.

These words the Team spake unto all Red Sox Nation, with a great voice over the loudspeaker: and they trembled, and said unto the Team, "So good! So good! So good!" And the Team wrote the commandments into two scoreboards and delivered them unto ye.

But these commandments have been held dear for many generations and mustn't be violated.

3,000 years old and was founded by the Canaanites, who were just looking for a bathhouse.

It was then destroyed during the Reformation of the 16th century and was built into a temple similar to what you see now. Of course, the giant wall in left field was built to keep the Conquistadors out. As you learned in the Architecture section, General Taylor and his son admired the blueprints found in the ruins and constructed a wall of their own (both kept out non-paying spectators). Also, guard towers stood where the light stanchions are today.

To protect the place of worship, different religions take different measures: the Jews place a mezuzah over the door; Catholics place a statue of Jesus; and Fenway has a statue of Ted Williams behind the park with a child praying at his feet. Millions of visitors to the Chapel every year take turns asking the statue for hitting lessons.

Inside the Chapel, we have activities that help us focus our attention on the holy.

Sacred Dances

These dances were originally reenactments of Christian deliverance from the powers of sin and death; now it's just fat people lifting their shirts to jiggle in time with the music in an attempt to get onto a highlight reel.

Music

There are four songs that are to be revered, never to be maligned, mocked, or played at inconsequential times. These songs bring people together. They signal a connection among nationals. And, as an added perk, they drive people from New York nuts every time they hear them. It's just another example of the religious power music possesses. These songs are important.

"Sweet Caroline"

This song is played during the eighth inning of all home games. It was going to be "You Don't Bring Me Flowers," but that was a duet and tougher to choreograph.

KEY TERMS

"the Kid" [da kid**]** *n*—the nickname for Red Sox great Ted Williams, he went on to have many kids of his own, including one that ended up freezing him

Archaeologists recently pillaged the Tomb of the Unknown Fan and found a scroll noting that the inspiration for this song was none other than Caroline Kennedy herself. She attended many games at Fenway as a youngster, a guest of her uncle's. Neil Diamond, a struggling singer/songwriter, was at the park on one of these occasions and happened to catch a glimpse of her in a lovely summer dress wearing a little bonnet and sucking on a rainbow all-day sucker. To him, she looked so dainty and pure that he just knew there was a song about her somewhere in the recesses of his mind.

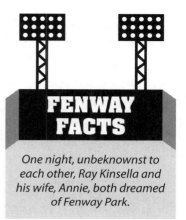

FENWAY FACTS

One night, unbeknownst to each other, Ray Kinsella and his wife, Annie, both dreamed of Fenway Park.

Then the umpire missed a stolen-base call at second base and Caroline stood up from her front-row seat and screamed, "Are you blind, ump?! He was safe! Ya ——!"

Neil was incredulous. All he could do was shake his head and say, "Sweet Caroline."

"Dirty Water"

Our anthem is played at Fenway Park after every Sox home win, and at least once an hour on every rock station in Boston as mandated by the governor. Ironically, the song itself is about getting mugged down by what was formerly the country's dirtiest waterway. (Contrary to popular belief, it is not paying tribute to what comes out of the concession stand taps at Fenway.)

We're proud of our anthem. We hear the song and scream, "Yep, that's us. I've been getting mugged and slimed down there for years. I love Boston!" At least Boston sees the irony. Los Angeles' anthem is "I Love L.A." by Randy Newman. Los Angelenos love it, but have no idea it's about how superficial they really are.

"Tessie"

When the first members of Red Sox Nation, the Royal Rooters, were just starting out as mere Peasant Rooters, they used the sounds of a familiar song, "Tessie," to disrupt the Pittsburgh Pirates in the first World Series.

The song was brought back to popularity in 2004 and redone by the Dropkick Murphys. Of course, the song is much different now than it was then:

> *Oh, Tessie, you're so fine*
> *You're so fine*
> *You blow my mind*
> *Hey, Tessie! [clap clap clap]*
> *Hey, Tessie! [clap clap clap]*

"I'm Shipping Up to Boston"

The Dropkick Murphys have their own song, too, and it's become synonymous with the celebration. The haunting deep bass, the drums, the twang of the banjo, and the sound of the accordion have become ensconced in the Boston culture. One note gets your feet to tapping. The song speaks to an entire city. There's not one inhabitant of Red Sox Nation who can't relate to these immortal words:

> *I'm a sailor peg*
> *And I've lost my leg*
> *Climbing up the top sails*
> *I lost my leg!*
> *I'm shipping up to Boston whooooa (3x)*
> *I'm shipping off...to find my wooden leg.*

No truer words have ever been spoken. Originally, the band encouraged their groupies to hold their wooden legs high in the air during the chorus, but this practice was discontinued at Fenway Park when fans began filling their wooden legs with beer and getting totally blitzed by the time Francona called for Papelbon.

Chants

Chanting is more than just words being repeated over and over monotonously. It is the ability to immediately summon up an army of like-minded individuals and outshout anyone not in agreement. It might be the most powerful demonstration of spirituality. Just a voice, a few words, and someone bold enough and loud enough to start it are needed.

Chanting is done in three different cadences. The first is your basic 1-2-3, where each beat is uniformly consistent with the other two. It is the scheme upon which the "Yankees suck!" chant is predicated. This cadence works for a variety of chants, including "MVP," "We love Youk," and "I want beer."

The second follows a more complex rhythm and adds clapping, which is a major part of many chants. It takes the basic 1-2-3 pattern, adds a 1-2 in the middle, and finishes with another 1-2-3 and two claps. The most popular of these is "Here we go, Red Sox, here we go! [clap clap]".

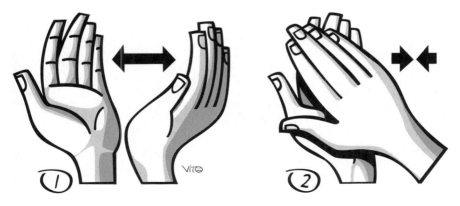

The final pattern is clap-heavy with a seesaw cadence. It's 1-2, 1-2, followed by a 1-2, 1-2-3 clap sequence, where the pitch of the 1 is high and the pitch of the 2 is low; for example, "Let's Go, Red Sox! [clap clap clapclapclap]". This one best suits the occasion when you're a mob moving in unison.

Feasts and Festivals

Food holds an important place in the lives of most Soxists. As is customary in most religions, there are dietary rules that list prohibited foods. Most food that comes from an that is acceptable. If meat is not chosen, there are other options, such as shellfish, but only if fried or served in a white broth, such as cream or milk. Little pieces of bacon and soup nuts are recommended, but not required.

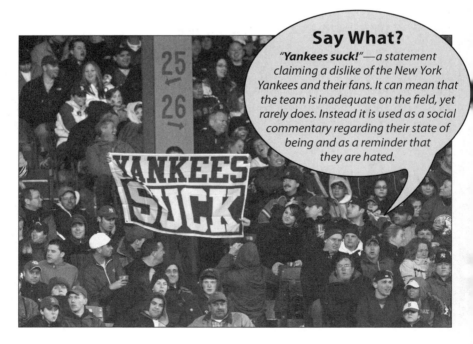

Say What?

"Yankees suck!"—a statement claiming a dislike of the New York Yankees and their fans. It can mean that the team is inadequate on the field, yet rarely does. Instead it is used as a social commentary regarding their state of being and as a reminder that they are hated.

Fenway Faithful [fen'way faithful] *n*—Red
Sox fans at Fenway Park; fans who stay until
the final out

KEY TERMS

Then there are items that come from no living creatures.
They must fall into two categories: those that contain the cheese
of a hoofed creature, such as pizza or a calzone, or that which
is infinitely salty and/or seasoned and starchy. A glazed caramel
topping is acceptable as well, but only if there's a surprise inside
like a miniature baseball card or a temporary tattoo.

Imitation animal products are forbidden, as are lower-fat
options such as the turkey, the buffalo, and the ostrich. If you
want that stuff, go to Whole Foods, not Fenway.

Beverage is a necessary accoutrement to the meal during
the Festival of the Innings. One might suggest a hops-laden
drink, sometimes malted, definitely wheat-based. Drinks with
bubbles are also acceptable if they include sugar and corn
syrup. Should water be your beverage of choice, be prepared
to produce a doctor's note detailing whatever medical condition you have that is preventing you from drinking one of your
primary options.

beer [beah] *n*—the life force through which
all activity happens; sustenance; a source
of nourishment; the cause of aggressive,
embarrassing, or foolish behavior

KEY TERMS

171

Ceremonial and Ritualistic Objects

Food is ingestible sacrament, but some objects are not meant to be ingested. (Lapel pins are not for eating.) A popular custom is to include paraphernalia in one's tradition.

Dr. Hector Chucklebutt penned the foremost dissertation on the subject of ceremonial and ritualistic objects. He broke down the various sacred items and their power to the practitioners.

Rally Cap

A rally cap is a scientifically proven method of game changing. The rally monkey, on the other hand, is a simian that scares you into cheering. If you refuse, he will bite you and give you Ebola.

The truth is, the rally monkey is actually an actor who doesn't care whether his team scores or not. Her real name is Katie. You might remember her as Marcel the Monkey on *Friends*. Yes, the fans in Anaheim follow an actor.

Now you might ask yourself, *Where can I get a rally cap? I've already spent $30 on a regular cap.*

It is a common misconception to believe you'll need a second cap, since all caps come rally-enabled, with a "rally" function. To activate, simply remove your hat

THEY SAID IT

"I can play first base, outfield, I sing karaoke in my underwear, and I'm a real selective hitter."

—*Kevin Millar, in a 2003 meeting with Red Sox brass*

and turn it inside out. Then replace it atop your head. Flipping the brim up acts as the power button. Once done, your rally cap is now "on."

Rally caps are to be donned only when runs are needed from the seventh inning on and the Red Sox are at bat. At all other times, it should be turned off, otherwise you will waste the karmic batteries.

Religious Statues and Images

These are viewed as the permanent embodiments of the deities they represent. One statue that was seen as critically important to our culture was the statue of Manny at home plate with his arms raised. (It's not really a statue, but rather videotaped footage of him pissing off opposing teams by showboating on most home runs.)

The famous statue of Ted Williams behind Fenway Park guards the field from evil spirits, while at the same time giving pigeons something to aim for.

Oh, Really?

Ted Williams (a.k.a. "the Kid," "Teddy Ballgame," "the Splendid Splinter," or "Theodore Samuel" to his mother whenever he did something wrong) was perhaps best known as one of only two players in major league history to steal a base in four different decades (Rickey Henderson is the other). Ted Williams was also a pretty good hitter. He's the last man to hit over .400 in one season, which means that for every four times he got a hit, he made six outs, so take that for what you will. He hit 521 homers in his day, even though he missed five years due to fighting in two different wars.

Ask the Valedictorian

Is it okay to leave the park during a blowout?

Red Sox fans have a reputation for being great fans, always there until the final out. Plus, we take great pride in pointing out how Yankee Stadium empties when their team is routed. But are we as loyal as we'd like to believe?

If the Sox are ahead or behind by an insurmountable number of runs, just ride the wave until the end. Punch out when it's quitting time and not any sooner.

However, weeknight games provide a problem for those with jobs or school the next day. RSU does not condone leaving early in the event of a blowout, but we won't expel you either. Just do it without any great fanfare. (Note: playoff games should never be abandoned, especially if the Sox are down seven runs to Tampa Bay.)

The Boston Sports Museum houses many less-revered sculptures, such as a bronze Kevin Millar singing karaoke in his underwear, a marble Jonathan Papelbon mid-*Riverdance*, and a wire statuette of Jerry Remy drag-bunting (housed in the Forgotten Fundamentals wing of the building).

FENWAY FACTS

Wally the Green Monster and his wife, Wilma, live in a gated community in the upscale town of Weston. He says the school district was a major selling point.

Amulets

The unwritten rule of Soxism is that one must make noise without accessories or props. The only item that may be exhibited in a wave-like motion include a hat (baseball, not cowboy or beanie), a banner revealing a salutary phrase such as, "Hi, Don and Jerry, Stockbridge says 'Woof!'" or, if you are under 12 years of age, a giant foam finger. Anything else is blasphemous. Those waving towels or foam tomahawks are looked upon as the sports fan equivalent of Carrot Top.

Amulets have fallen out of favor in baseball ever since the magic amulet used by the Kansas City Royals in the 1983 World Series made their bench coach disappear. Still, many fans of other major league teams incorporate them into their religions, and it behooves Red Sox fans to be aware of them.

Towels

Some fans wave their white laundry in the air during games in an attempt to intimidate the opposing team, but to the rest of us it just looks like they're declaring, "Surrender!" Hankies, towels, rags, whatever you'd like to call them, are bandied about with more fervor than you'd use on your own child for winning a spelling bee.

Twins fans wave their Homer Hankies after dressing up as Sox fans for Halloween.

thunder sticks [lame invenshuns] *n*— inflatable tubes that, when banged together, identify the most annoying fans in the world

Tomahawks

Another object used to funnel positive energy toward a team is the tomahawk. It was ceremonial in the mid-19th century to take a real tomahawk to the opposing team's starting pitcher. This was before they had laws regarding this sort of behavior. Back then, they placed a lot more importance on recreational activities than they did on the importance of human life.

Noisemakers

The fairly recent invention of **thunder sticks** has led to fans across the country banging them together like Jolly Chimps. These sticks are more likely to cause the person using the sticks to be hit, however. When a thunder-sticking group of fans is outnumbered, the sticks are often shoved where the sun doesn't shine (otherwise known as a **California wedgie**) midway through the game once the sound becomes unbearable.

Some fan bases choose one representative to make the noise for the entire group. For example, this person might pound a big drum steadily during the game. It is done until it starts to rain. This allows their starting pitchers to get plenty of off days as the field is constantly deluged. Depending on the methodical rhythm

California wedgie [kalifournya wedgy] *n*— what you should give anyone using thunder sticks

created, it has been known to bring snow in April, fog in June, and bugs (of the Biblical variety) in October, though the bugs may only have been attracted to the Yankees' hefty set-up man and come on their own. One thing the drumming has not been found to cause, however, is winning.

All of these objects are strictly taboo in Red Sox Nation. On one muggy June night, Dave Wolthoff was sitting in the bleachers and took a towel out just to wipe his forehead. He was promptly shoved into the Jimmy Fund donation box. It was not as bad as it seemed, though, as he was tax deductible.

Prayers

Prayer is the No. 1 pastime in all of Red Sox Nation. Most people use the ritual of prayer to get through the "emotional valleys." And they have a full arsenal at their disposal, with prayers for every occasion that they may encounter.

Petition

In all of sports, this prayer is used most frequently. It is when you simply request a material or spiritual gift, be it a home run or the strength to forgive another passed ball:

Please let him get a hit, o Lord, for thou art the most wise and benevolent ruler...and handsome, too.

KEY TERMS

walk-off [wok awf] *n*—a game-ending home run, resulting in the winning team proudly pounding the hero on the head at home plate until he can no longer remember his own name

Confession

This affirms your faith and acknowledges your state of sin:

I admit that I was wrong when I said there was "no way" the Sox would blow an eight-run lead. I beg your forgiveness and promise it will never happen again.

> ### HAIL PAPI
>
> *Hail Papi full of grace,*
> *The Lord is with Thee,*
> *Blessed art thou among power hitters*
> *Blessed is the fruit of thy swing*
> *Holy Papi, King of Walk-Offs, pray*
> *For us sinners now and at the bottom*
> *Of the ninth. Amen.*

I am sorry that I stole that Slushee from the 7-Eleven. I know you work in mysterious ways, but I didn't expect you to penalize me by making the Sox lose four straight. Couldn't I have just said three "Hail Papis" instead?

Intercession

The needs of others are expressed in this type of prayer:

Please, father, giveth him the curveball with enough bite that it doth evade the swing of the interloper's bat.

Father, forgive him, for he knows not what he does in yanking the pitcher after only five innings.

Praise and Thanksgiving

These are two separate methods of prayer. Praise redeems the mystical experience of prayer by celebrating God himself, not for his works, but for himself, his greatness and mystery; really, just because He's a pretty cool dude. In essence, you're sucking up. This should be done

> ### Say What?
>
> *"**Believe!**"—formerly a state of unreality causing millions of people to think something impossible could be done. Now it indicates a willingness to watch every inning and every game in October and think positive thoughts even in the face of great adversity.*

routinely. Remember, if you show up only when you need something, He's going to know.

Thanksgiving celebrates God's deeds. This is a real favorite of the players themselves.

> *Interviewer:* That was a clutch pitch you threw there in the ninth.
>
> *Religious Athlete:* Yeah, it was. I wanna thank God for helping me make it....

Meanwhile, players on the other team are shaking their heads and wondering, *How could God do that to us?* Many times, this prayer is accompanied by fireworks or perhaps a person sliding down a chute into a giant vat of beer. It might be done for the fans, but we know who it's really for.

Adoration

The most seldom-used of all prayers, it is also the noblest. It is a prostration of the whole being before God. It's a submissive reverence shown by body movements: raising the hands, a deep bowing of the body, and a kneeling with hand to mouth, forehead to the ground.

Oh, Lord, I am but a small flea on the dog of life and am not worthy to be in your presence yada yada yada.

RED SOX DEITIES

Over the years, Red Sox fans have found salvation through an extensive list of deities, each with a specialized purpose:

Fisk—the God of Dramatic Finishes

Boggs—the God of Hits

Dewey—the God of Rifles

Youkilis—the God of Walks

Papi—the God of Walk-Offs

Roberts—the God of Steals

Morgan—the God of Magic

Petey—the God of Fatherhood

Beckett—the God of Playoffs

Pap—Lord of the Dance

Yaz—the God of Dreams

Schilling—the God of Gritty Performances

Feller—the God of Introductions

Kiley—the God of Organ Music

Ned—the God of Mercy

Usually this comes after several memorable moments and many beers. Three million people along a parade route used this one day in October a few years ago and again in 2007.

Trade-Off

This final prayer is very businesslike. You are, in essence, entering into a contract with your god: "If you do this, Lord, I will do that." An informal study by the Center for Informal Studies came to the conclusion that the most renounced activity in these arrangements is drinking. However, only 3 percent of all promises involving drinking are kept.

Coming in second is giving up one's spouse and/or child. This has been dramatized in the now famous fake commercial spoofing MasterCard, where creditors come to collect on all the trade-offs made during the Red Sox's playoff run in 2004. To Denis Leary, a creditor reads from a transcript, "You said, and I quote, 'I'd give my left nut to have the Sox win the Series.'" Always the dutiful gambler, Mr. Leary acquiesces and allows them to collect.

Emphasis on Sacrifice

Red Sox Nation does not put much emphasis on sacrifice. The act of placing an object at the altar to appease the gods hasn't been used since Martin Perry. In early 1997, frustrated by the Red Sox's futility during his lifetime, Martin brought his youngest son, Maxwell, to the Fenway box office in the hopes of leaving him there for the gods to accept (or at least to get season tickets in exchange). He figured he had three sons of whom he was proud, but no championship team, so he would gladly trade one son for the latter.

The trade was rejected by the box office and Maxwell was eventually returned to Martin before Child Services came and took

LOOKING THE PART

Rituals can be enacted in any way, but using religious dress and vestments can enhance many rituals. Dress can include a wide range of attire from T-shirts to game shirts to long-sleeve shirts to fleece shirts to three-quarter shirts to shirts over shirts. Then there are tattoos (the "B" in a Red Sox font, or a pair of socks), or markings (a birthmark in the shape of Luis Tiant). Face and body paint can also be incorporated (colors should be in reds and blues only, and it is not recommended that you wear them when driving through gang territory).

him away. Maxwell, meanwhile, pooled his paper route money with his older siblings and they bought season tickets back when they were still available. The trio was front and center for the 2004 World Series, sending their father photos after the fact.

These days, the only ritualistic sacrifice seems to be a food drive held by the Jimmy Fund as you enter the park. Just drop your canned goods into the boxes. It might not bring the team success, but it is good for your karma and good for the charity.

Life and Death

Here is where religion begins to entangle itself with philosophy. Can any of these prayers and rituals cheat death? Perhaps it seems as if they can't, but if you look at the gods as all-powerful, all-knowing, and having too much time on their hands, it might just be that they have a plan that stretches beyond the current moment.

"Death," in this instance, is the end of the baseball season or, more specifically, the end of the Red Sox's season. Red Sox fans are constantly haunted by the prospect of death. It materializes in September, October, and some years as early as July.

Elimination from the playoffs—sometimes called "Dia de los Muertes"—segues from life to death, initiating a mourning period that can last up to four months. The mourner's prayer consists of a *minyan* (at least 10 people) quietly chanting, "Next year, next year, next year, next year..." until their spouses throw them out of the house. Some people choose to hold the ceremony over an open grave, where they can throw all their paraphernalia from the season into it and then chase it with a match.

Acceptance allows for the realization that the spring will bring another team with the hopes and dreams instilled in them by this great Nation. But there are people who maintain the non-acceptance of death as the definitive end of life. "Maybe the commissioner's office will review the series and find a loophole," they say. "The Sox can still win the wild-card if Minnesota decides to disband their franchise before the playoffs," they wish. These people have issues.

Fear of the Dead

Mystics constantly point to that which is dead as the cause for many of a team's trials. The belief that forces beyond this earth pull so much weight in determining the future is, on the outside, ludicrous. But when one believer convinces another and he does the same and so on and so forth, you have society treating a belief as a given. Adults will be at the will of the dead, doing what they can to appease the ghost. They might dig up a piano that had allegedly been thrown into a pond or make a foul ball smack off the face of a child who was currently living in what was once the home of the spirit. (That last one seems to work, by the way.) Either way, the populace, as reasonable as they seem, finds themselves at the mercy of the dead.

Each religion follows its own legend. One particular congregation in the Midwest fears a goat. How silly is that?

Ask the Valedictorian

When should a Red Sox fan hit the "panic button"?

The panic button is not to be trifled with. It is a device to be used only in the direst of circumstances. Treat it responsibly. (Before you hit it, you must remember to rid your home of any sharp objects and dangerous chemicals.)

If glaring holes have been exposed in the team dynamic and the trading deadline has passed, you might decide you want to press the panic button. If the offense shuts down or the pitching becomes suspect during one or more games in a playoff series, the panic button is a definite option. If injuries begin to mount in a catastrophically bad way, the panic button is your only friend.

On the other hand, if the Yankees come to town and their fans begin to play keep-away with your pants, well, then the panic button can't really help you.

After a season's death, it is time to eliminate the evil spirits that haunt your clothing, possessions, and property. There are several reasons why this must take place. First of all, if there was a long winning streak and you refrained from doing laundry, your clothing smells so bad that you must purify it to keep the neighbors from complaining. Another common belief is that your possessions were a meeting place for the bad luck and you must essentially destroy that place. It's the idea that a fresh start can only be achieved if all connections to the past are erased.

Some fans routinely change their name after a season ends. It takes roughly four months to get all your credit cards and identification up to date for the new season. Then one freak injury to Big Papi and you'll have to do it all over again come fall.

Another option is to obtain new friends or a different family to, in essence, change your identity. It also makes it seem like you've been reincarnated; you have the same soul, but a different vessel in which to travel (though perhaps a vessel with the same gimpy back when it rains).

At a minimum, you should perform the quintessential purification ritual and take a hot shower to expunge the smell of beer and wings you've absorbed from 162 straight days at the bar.

The Afterlife

It could be that like Bruce Willis' character in *The Sixth Sense,* we're already dead but don't know it yet. (If that ruined the ending for anyone, it's your own fault, as you should've seen it by now.) Winning twice in four years after thinking it would never happen? Doesn't that seem a little odd? Could we have died and this is all taking place in heaven? If that's the case, how do you explain the Bruins? Why would such a beloved team wallow in such misfortune year after year if we were in heaven?

This is a discussion for a more advanced course. But just imagine what heaven would be like. Dwight Evans would be in the Hall of Fame. Ted Williams would have a championship ring. O.J. Simpson would be getting pistol-whipped by a long line of beaten wives out for revenge. What's heaven like for you?

The late author Cleveland Amory once said, "we could never be a Yankee fan because we would win too much. And if you win too much, you will not go to heaven. The Bostonian will go to heaven because he has suffered too much here. You must suffer in this life, and then you will go directly to heaven."

There you have it—if there are Yankees fans around you, then you are not in heaven. Glad we got that straightened out.

Summary

The beliefs and practices of Soxism, followed by an entire society, make up the culture in which we live; strange to others, but all too normal to us. It kind of makes you see how people can be crazy enough to follow Scientology. (If you are a Scientologist, we mean "crazy" like "crazy cool" and the University would like to thank you for your purchase of this textbook.)

RED SOX

Fun at the Park

Play "Uniform-Number Bingo." Don't use numbers; rather, use the names of the players who wear/wore those numbers. (For example, "B–Jim Rice" would be "B–14" and "N–Jason Varitek" would be "N–33.")

Test Your Knowledge

How do you deal with loss?

When is it time to stop believing?

Who but W.B. Mason?

A home-run ball you catch should always be:
   (A) thrown back if it was hit by the visiting team
   (B) given to a kid (unless he's a Yankees fan)
   (C) slept with that night
   (D) held up for all to see
   (E) sold on eBay

What should you do if you see a *Monbouquette*?
   (A) see a doctor to get rid of it
   (B) get it appraised
   (C) alert the media and take a photograph
   (D) shake its hand and greet it with a smile
   (E) pin it to your date like a corsage

The smell of Fenway or the smell of a newborn baby's head—which do you like better?

Graduation

This completes your undergraduate education at Red Sox University. Do you feel smarter now than you did when you started? Have new fans learned the ropes? Have longtime fans received a fresh dose of knowledge? We certainly hope so; if not, sorry, no refunds.

Now that you have mastered our strict curriculum, please do not get cocky and raise your proverbial arms before the ball has left the yard. Yes, you can grasp such simple concepts as the wave, you can deduce what possible reason the team has for playing the backup second baseman even though he can't hit, you're familiar with 1986, and you can keep pace with what's happening in the present, but there is still much to be learned.

Graduate classes will allow you to branch out into the areas of fandom that most interests you. You might want to look into Global Economics—how to budget a road trip to another ballpark; Spanish—conversing with the home team's fans when the Red Sox visit Miami or Los Angeles; and Speech Communication—talking to Yankees fans in a civil and mature manner. But for now, just enjoy your Bachelor's of Sox (BS) degree.

Do not be afraid of what the future holds for you, for you are Red Sox fans, the most resilient of all fans. If you put your mind to something, there's nothing you cannot overcome, whether it be a 3-0 deficit in the playoffs or two barren years without a championship. You will always have your beliefs by your side.

Thank you for matriculating at Red Sox University. If you've enjoyed learning half as much as the faculty has enjoyed teaching you, then the faculty has enjoyed teaching you twice as much as you've enjoyed learning.

And, of course, "Go Sox!"

Acknowledgments

First off, I'd like to thank everyone who directly helped with and influenced the creation of this book, including the entire staff at Triumph Books, who were impressive with their professionalism and gave an author everything he could need. Special mention goes to my editor Adam Motin; illustrator Vito Sabsay; Sue Knopf, who handled the layout and design; and Tom Bast for seeing the potential of this project.

Then there are the people I want to thank for their indispensible, if not necessarily obvious, assistance during the creative process. Patrick Freeman, who deftly helps me improve every project; Adam Pearlman, for being my doppelganger and Red Sox Nation presidential campaign advisor; former Red Sox pitcher Rich "El Guapo" Garces for letting me be him for an evening back in 2007; Jason Gold, who's a Yankees fan and really doesn't deserve anything but a hot dog with mustard on it in the face, save for the fact that he's constantly trying to get me in with the big boys; Jimmy Pitaro, for his attempts to promote me; Jeff Louderback, for allowing me to write on Soxandpinstripes.com; Chuck Burgess, for being a great peer to know and emulate; John Rinaldo, for creative discussions; Sol Nasisi, for his help in advertising; Scott Russell, for his "insanity" and love of the game; Doug Strasnick and Michelle Oberfell, for their legal advice and friendship; Steve "Tweed Coat" Hanna and "Wild Wild" Wes Newman, for supporting me and letting me disappear for months at a time; my cousin, Jonathan, for being my biggest promoter; Nick Benas, for being such a good friend, adviser, and fellow passenger on this little raft ride we're on going straight to the top of the cream soda we call life; and all the baseball fans, Red

Sox and otherwise, I've had the pleasure and privilege to meet and speak to along the way, including Brewers fan Bob Buchta, to whom I owe a beer.

Finally, I'd like to give an extra special thanks (though thanks cannot accurately describe my feelings) to my family, most notably my mother, Roberta, and sister, Sue, for their constant emotional support during the stressful times. As always, go Sox!

About the Author

Andy Wasif has been a Red Sox fan since the days of skipper Ralph Houk. He attended Syracuse University's Newhouse School of Public Communications with an eye on sports journalism. Graduation brought him to Los Angeles, where he spent time as a stand-up comedian. Fully recovered from that profession, the Boston native now shuttles back and forth between the Northeast and Southern California, working on television and film projects including *The Diary of Gunkie Malloy*. His other books include *How to Talk to a Yankee Fan* with coauthor Rick D'Elia and *Not the Life for Me*.